Greatcoats and Glamour Boots

940
.53
15042
0971
Gos

Gossage, Carolyn, 1933-
  Greatcoats and glamour boots : Canadian women at
war (1939-1945) / Carolyn Gossage. -- Toronto :
Dundurn Press, 1991.
  215 p. : ill.

Includes bibliographical references (p. [213-215])
06033458   ISBN:1550020951 (pbk.)

1. Canada. Royal Canadian Air Force. Women's Division.
2. Canada. Canadian Army. Canadian Women's Army
Corps. 3. Canada. Royal Canadian Navy. Women's Royal
(SEE NEXT CARD)

6126   91DEC12   th/   1-00982568

Greatcoats and Glamour Boots

Canadian Women at War (1939–1945)

CAROLYN GOSSAGE

Dundurn Press
Toronto & Oxford
1991

Copy Editor: Doris Cowan
Design: JAQ
Production: Eva Payne
Printing and Binding: Gagné Printing Ltd., Louiseville, Quebec, Canada

Dundurn Press wishes to acknowledge the generous assistance and ongoing support of **The Canada Council, The Book Publishing Industry Development Programme** of the **Department of Communications** and **The Ontario Arts Council.**
    Care has been taken to trace the ownership of copyright material used in the text, including the illustrations. The author and publisher welcome any information enabling them to rectify any reference or credit in subsequent editions.

J. Kirk Howard, Publisher

Canadian Cataloguing in Publication Data

Gossage, Carolyn, 1933–
    Greatcoats and glamour boots

Includes bibliographical references.
ISBN 1-55002-095-1

1. Canada. Royal Canadian Air Force. Women's
Division. 2. Canada. Canadian Army. Canadian
Women's Army Corps. 3. Canada. Royal Canadian Navy.
Women's Royal Canadian Naval Service. 4. World
War, 1939–1945 – Participation, Female. I. Title.

D810.W7G68 1991   940.5315'042'0971   C91–094671–X

Dundurn Press Limited
2181 Queen Street East
Suite 301
Toronto, Canada
M4E 1E5

Dundurn Distribution
73 Lime Walk
Headington
Oxford, England
OX3 7AD

For "Aunt Snubbie"

Nancy Leigh Gossage Eaton

A wartime Wren whose enduring courage is much admired

Contents

	Acknowledgments	9
	Foreword	12
	Introduction	16
One	Onward and Upward: The Pre-Mobilization Years (1938–1941)	21
Two	Joining Up	35
Three	Preparing to Serve	71
Four	All in Together, Girls	111
Five	On Duty at Home and Overseas	149
Six	Off Duty	181
Seven	Phasing Out	193
	Notes	207
	Related Sources	213

ACKNOWLEDGMENTS

As my dear old Grandmother Curtis used to say, "It's never over till it's over." Now, at long last, I can extend my appreciation and thanks to those who contributed in one way or another to making this book a reality.

Much of the research for this book was made possible through grants from the Canada Council and the Ontario Arts Council. In addition I am grateful for the unqualified co-operation of the staff of the Directorate of History, National Defence Headquarters in Ottawa. In particular I would like to thank Brereton Greenhous, senior historian; W.A.B. Douglas, director; and Phillip Chaplin for their personal interest and encouragement. I am also indebted to Dr. Jean Cottam for providing extensive information on Soviet women in combat.

My appreciation is extended, as well, to Terresa McIntosh of the National Archives of Canada for all her help in connection with Molly Lamb Bobak's war diaries and to Carole Weisbrod of the Canadian War Museum. At the Canadian Forces Photographic Unit, the assistance given by Janet Lacroix and Raymond Gagnon was also truly gratifying, as was that of Felicia Cukier of the Art Gallery of Ontario's Photographic Services.

I am especially indebted to Caird F. Wilson for her patience in attempting to impart computer keyboarding skills to the semi-literate and for the countless hours she spent putting the bulk of the manuscript onto disk; also to David J. Wood for his efforts and for the use of his IBM P.C. during my first tentative ventures into computerland.

The research for this book has been a truly co-operative effort. The encouragement and assistance given me by Catherine Shepard of the Archives of Ontario are inestimable, as is the hospitality extended to me by Helen Murphy et al. , during my frequent and often lengthy stays in

Ottawa. To Carlyn Moulton for her enthusiasm and advice, many thanks. I am most grateful, as well, to Joan Chalmers and Pat Patterson for their help in arranging interviews with a number of former Canadian servicewomen and to Carol Martin for endorsing my original proposal to undertake the research for this book. Marian Engel, too, was extremely supportive from the outset. We miss her.

Beyond this there are legions of friends, relations and total strangers who have been instrumental in making this book possible. The following is only a partial list of those to whom I am indebted for interviews, conversations and letters; for sharing their photos, scrapbooks and their wartime reminiscences. Sadly a number of those whose names appear below have passed away in the intervening years.

Marg Ackroyd, Jessie Allen, Phyllis Arnoldi, Grace Arrell, Hélène L'Espérance Baldwin, Mary E. Barker, Janet Barr Beames, Anne-Marie Bélanger, Doreen Bennett, Audrey Bouler, Betty Legg Brown, Mona Kennerley Brown, Edith Bruckland, Mary Buch, Margaret Clark, Sherry Close, Margaret "Pat" Cooke, Beatrice Grant Corbett, Gwen Crawford, Isabel Cronyn, Rachel Crossey, Enid Hunt Dahl, Dorothy H. Davis, Isabel Davis, Jessie Cameron Deresno, Connie Duncan, Margaret Eaton Dunn, Barbara Cole Feiden, Helen Hunt Ford, Margot Frazier, Frances Gage, Al Gasparini, Tony German, Mabel Glaser, Bunnie O'Donnell Graf, C. Graham, Ruth Grant, Peggy Gray, Nan Gregg, Frances Hallis, Alfred Hanson, O.G. Heck, Shirley Heesaker, Claire Loranger Heise, Marguerite Hill, Mary Eileen Hogg, C.M., Gordon J. Hopkins, Mary Fairclough Houston, Nancy Gigot Hughson, Jean Huston, Jean Jamieson, Lois Johnston, Tracy Johnston, Donald Kidd, Elizabeth Madigan Kilbride, Helen King, Rosemary Kowalsky, Edwin Michael Lally, Ruby Lang, Barbara Lee, Susan Leggat, Betty MacDonald, Joy MacDonald, Lena Stevenson MacGillivray, Betty MacLean, Ruth McCullough Markowitz, Florence McAleese, Lillian K. McCullough, Hilda B. McMartin, Eva Miller, Anne Mitchell, Phyllis Montagnon, Norma Law Morrow, Thelma Thompson Murdoch, Margot Murray, Lois Anthony Norr, M.W. "Pat" Patterson, Barbara Good Power, Henrietta Rea, Jennie Lee Ricketts, Margaret Roach, Lillian Roe, Grace Rose, Jill Rosling, Shelagh Rounthwaite, Ann Rowe, Lillian Rowe Helen Rutherford, Charmaine Samson Scott, Martha Scott, Georgie Ridout Seeley, Marjorie Seeton, Marie Battle Shadgett, Brian Sheppard, Marg Sheppard, Agnes I. Shreve, Betty Simone, Jean Skoggard, Joy Dunham

Smith, Lee Thirwall, Elizabeth Titus, Margaret M. Toth, "Pat" Vaisey, Barbara Walker, Mabel Ware, Wayne Warwick, Lottie Watson, Lorna Mary West, Agnes Wezner, Margaret Wallace-Whatley, Owen S. Williams, Mildred Young, Nora Young.

And finally to MBG, Valerie and Graeme for their ongoing support along the way, the "Hoover" extends thanks beyond measure.

CMG

FOREWORD

NOT LONG AFTER I HAD begun the research for this book, I discovered that my efforts had come under fire. A woman who had previously held an impressive military rank during the Second World War let it be known that in her view no one who had not actually experienced wartime service in uniform could possibly write about it with any validity. Who did I think I was? How could a gormless civilian begin to grasp the patriotic significance of it all? In this she was probably correct. It *is* virtually impossible, since my own recollections of those years differ vastly from those of someone who signed up "for the duration." Mine was the sidelines generation – old enough to remember, but too young to take an active part.

My first awareness of "the war" was the sound of my mother sobbing, while in the background, crackling through the tubes of our Rogers Majestic radio, I could hear a voice – the ranting staccato of a moustachioed little housepainter grown powerful – proclaiming the might of his Third Reich, which would soon bring the world to its knees. It was September 1939. I was six, and Canada was at war.

Gradually new words and phrases found their way into my burgeoning vocabulary: wartime expressions like "ditty bag," "War Savings stamps" and "Victory Bonds." The grownups often talked about them, or about someone's being "on the Indian list" (drinking a lot). "Ration cards" were often mentioned, too, and a place called "The Canteen."

My mother spent a lot of time at the canteen doing dishes and it sounded like a very boring and horrible way for her to "contribute to the war effort" (her words), while I was farmed out to a friend's mother, protesting (no doubt obnoxiously) that I didn't want to play with Marianne. What I really meant, of course, was that I didn't want my mother to leave me. But it was all in the name of patriotism and I would simply have to try to understand.

Somehow I failed to attain that kind of wisdom, but new experiences increased my prepubescent consciousness of the fact that somewhere, far away, there was a war going on. And besides acquiring a wartime vocabulary, I developed new musical interests. My best friend's mother played the piano. She and her sister were entertainers and often she would be away "playing for the boys." When she was at home, though, there would be parties, and the guests, almost all of them in uniform, would be talking and chinking glasses and smoking like chimneys . . . The room seemed alive with carefree laughter and invariably there would be a group clustered around the piano in the dining room singing. "The White Cliffs of Dover" was very popular. Also "I'll Be Seeing You," "Coming In on a Wing and a Prayer" and my greatest delight, even then, "The North Atlantic Squadron," probably because the words were a little off-colour and certainly not considered suitable for a small girl's innocent ears. Only years afterwards did I discover that the North Atlantic Squadron belonged not to the Air Force, as I had imagined, but to His Majesty's Royal Canadian Navy.

Fairly early in the war, I received my first introduction to a blackout. An exciting sensation, not a frightening one, since my mother had prepared me well in advance. It was "just pretend" she assured me. Nothing was going to happen, really. It was just a way of making sure that people would know what to do if ever there were a real air raid. As soon as the sirens went off, we would scurry around shutting off all the lights, except for one small lamp in the living room. Then we'd draw all the curtains over the windows, so tightly that not one glimmer of light could be seen by the air raid warden when he made his rounds. Altogether an exciting game!

Unbeknownst to my mother, I played other games as well, secret ones, with my co-conspirator Teddy, the boy next door, whose bedroom was just across the alleyway from mine. Across this chasm we had rigged up an undetected telegraph line and at night, after we'd both been put to bed, we'd creep to our sets and begin sending out urgent messages to each other in Morse code, using the tiny flashing light intended for silent transmission. It was quite some time before our clandestine activities were uncovered and the sets confiscated till further notice. As spies we had outlived our usefulness.

Later on, when Harris, a good friend of the family who was a pilot in the Royal Canadian Air Force, was posted to Egypt, the war came a little closer for me. Harris was my idol; he smiled down at me from the picture that hung by my bed, jaunty in his pilot officer's uniform, and every night I said a special prayer to God to keep him safe and to please make sure he didn't get shot down or killed. By day, I hounded the postman for aerogram letters addressed to me.

Because of the shortage of gasoline during the war years, my mother and I took the train whenever we travelled any distance from Toronto. Usually it was to Montreal, to visit my grandparents. The train would always be bursting at the seams with people in uniform, smoking, drinking, playing cards, and of course singing. During the Christmas holidays we travelled by train to Collingwood, and again, the train was always full of khaki-uniformed men bound for Camp Borden. The conductor would call out, "Next stop, Angus!" and within minutes the train would seem strangely silent, with only a handful of passengers left, staring out the windows at the soldiers' backs as they sifted off down the platform before the train moved off into the night.

I can remember pressing my nose against the cold pane, watching them too, and wondering what it would be like to be a soldier and march behind a band. It never occurred to me then that some of those soldiers would be killed or wounded or taken prisoner. For the time being, that was beyond my understanding.

After my mother took a full-time job, I was packed off to boarding school in the country. There I found a few other girls who felt the call of duty, and we formed our own little ersatz female corps. A First World War drill manual that someone had foraged from the family attic proved to be an invaluable source of instruction. This was an elite corps, of course. Not just anybody could join. There was an oath to be pledged and a weekly fee to be donated to the Red Cross and you had to be willing to follow orders. Nor was it an easy feat to become an officer in our army. Not unexpectedly, there was a certain amount of bickering about who would give the orders and who would take them until we, the founders, ever mindful of the principles of democracy, agreed that the solution would be to take turns as commander-in-chief. Occasionally there would be deserters (we called them traitors), who were subsequently accorded the cold shoulder as only ten-year-old girls can deliver it.

The school, though somewhat remote from the real world, did its level best to help make us aware of the war effort. In class we were allotted time to knit squares for an afghan or to create string washcloths (my undoing) to go into sailors' ditty bags; and each of us had a little booklet, into which we dutifully stuck our War Savings stamps every Friday during "Red Cross time." Every spring we planted Victory gardens. Having been charged with a tiny plot, each of us tended our little piece of real estate, some of us with more zeal and loving care than others. (The harvest from mine was never bountiful, I'm afraid.)

In the autumn, when the milkweed pods were full and dry, we'd be taken out into the fields to collect them in burlap sacks. The milkweed would be used, we were told, to fill life jackets. Was it true, I wonder? It was never long until the air was awhirl with tiny silken parachutes and filled with girlish laughter. The war, for us, was very far away.

And when it was all finally over and the jubilation of VE-Day and VJ-Day had come and gone, nothing seemed very different. Life was about to embrace me; I was a post-war teenager who never gave a backward glance to the war years. Perhaps at the time I felt a twinge of disappointment that I was too young to have been a part of it, to have worn a uniform and marched behind a band. I really don't remember.

There are, however, many women still living who recall those years vividly. This book is for them – the women who enlisted and served in the Canadian Women's Army Corps, the RCAF Women's Division, and the Women's Royal Canadian Naval Service (better known as the Wrens), the women who accomplished "everything under the sun and then some . . . " It is dedicated, as well, to their remembered joys and sorrows, to "the experience of a lifetime" for those women who answered the call of duty and were never the same again.

Molly Lamb Bobak, *CWACs Relaxing*, ca. 1943.

INTRODUCTION

Canada has always been an unmilitary nation.
In time of peace the people have never shown much
inclination to prepare for war.
          — G.W. Nicholson[1]

IN OUR ALMOST BREATHLESS QUEST for a definitive national identity, it is doubtful that most Canadians would even consider the term militaristic as a compelling aspect of our heritage or character. For one thing, Canada's military history, at least from the popular viewpoint, is decidedly short on heroic figures (Laura Secord and Billy Bishop notwithstanding). But then, this apparent lack of identification with hero/heroine figures may be yet another underlying aspect of our national psyche. In any event, this is not intended as an incisive probing into the vagaries and complexities of the Canadian character. It is, rather, an attempt to document a relatively unknown reality.

Much has already been committed to print concerning the war years from every imaginable vantage point, but there is still at least one significant gap: some missing footage that this book will attempt to record. During the Second World War more than over 45,000 Canadian women volunteered for military service in the name of King and Country. Close to 22,000 of them enlisted in the CWAC (Canadian Women's Army Corps), 17,000 in the RCAF (Royal Canadian Air Force) Women's Division (WD), and 6,781 in the "Wrens" (Women's Royal Canadian Naval Service). With the notable exception of the 3,141 nursing sisters serving in Canada and overseas as officers in the Canadian Medical Corps during the First World War, there was virtually no female presence, in the military sense at least, until the Second World War; in fact, the Second World War had been under way for close to two years before Canadian women were finally given the option of active participation as enlisted members of the Canadian armed forces. The result was the creation of an entirely new wrinkle in the fabric of Canada's military history.

While it is true that the First World War gave many Canadian women the opportunity to serve their country, it was in a restricted and generally conventional manner, primarily as nursing sisters or volunteer workers in various organizations both at home and overseas. Eventually, as a manpower shortage developed, many more women joined the work force as munitions workers in Canadian factories. Initially, however, their role was well within the confines of tradition. During the "war to end all wars" and for some time to come, the notion of the female as a nurturing presence held sway. And, in fact, at the outset of the First World War even the necessity of recruiting nursing sisters was seriously questioned by at least one high-ranking member of Canada's military establishment. "Active service work is extremely severe," maintained Col. Guy Carleton Jones, "and a large portion of R.N.s are totally unfit for it, mentally or physically."[2] His conviction of their unsuitability proved to be entirely unfounded. By late 1918, 328 of these "unfit" persons had been decorated by George V; 50 had received foreign decorations; 169 had been mentioned in dispatches; and 46 had given their lives.[3]

The perseverance and devotion of Canada's nursing sisters through every imaginable vicissitude, not only in Britain, but in France, Belgium, the eastern Mediterranean, Egypt, and even Russia, were inestimable. Virtually without complaint they endured air raids, falling shrapnel, stifling heat, bone-chilling dampness, rain, sleet, mud, and more mud. They also bore witness to acute pain and suffering as well as indescribable courage, surrounded as they were on all sides by death and disease.

"There are two courages," wrote one of these nursing sisters while serving in France, "that of the mind, which is great; and that of the heart, which is greatest . . . There is a terrible sameness in war hospitals. There are rows of beds and in them rows of unshaven white-faced men. Some of them turn and look at visitors, others lie very still with their eyes fixed on the ceiling for Eternity or God knows what. Now and then one is sleeping. Often they die. If there is a screen, the death takes place decently and in order, away from the eyes of the ward. But when there is none, it makes little difference. What is one death to men who have seen so many? . . . They are all awaiting death or maybe home and health again . . ."[4]

Another describing the grim business of war expressed her own uneasy impressions: "This war has shown that government by men only is not an appeal to reason but an appeal to arms . . . It has shown that on women – without a word of protest – the burden must rest.[5]

The tireless efforts of the many women who flocked overseas as volunteers in the Canadian Red Cross, the YWCA (Young Women's Christian Association), the IODE (Imperial Order of the Daughters of the Empire), and the St. John Ambulance, among others, also deserve mention in the annals of a war that broke many precedents for women as well as men. The glimmer of a new concept of women's abilities to adapt themselves to almost any need comes through in this observation concerning the work of Canadian Red Cross workers overseas. Today its tone has a distinctly patronizing ring, but its sincerity at the time cannot be questioned: "We are all ready to give credit to women for tender sympathy but did we ever think women were capable of organizing such extensive undertakings?"[6]

And in factories and machine shops more and more women had been busily manufacturing the necessary equipment for the waging of war. Guns, fuses and shell were all in urgent demand and manpower was at a premium. The "zestful labours" of these female munitions workers did not go unrecognized:

> It has been clearly demonstrated that women, under the guidance of trained toolmakers are efficient and useful . . . Especially have women astonished engineers in their aptitude for the handling of milling machines. Twelve months ago no thought of woman labour was in the mind of any manufacturer. Experience has now proved that there is no operation on shellwork that a woman cannot do – and, as a matter of fact is doing – even to the heavy operations which require great physical strength. Proper selection of female labour makes this work equally suitable for women.[7]

Clearly, the efforts of all these individuals both overseas and in Canada amounted to "splendid work by splendid women" (the admiring observation of a postwar politician). However splendid they may have been, aside from the nursing sisters, who had been officially attached to the Canadian Army, women's involvement was essentially non-military in nature and would remain so until well into the Second World War. This was, of course, neither by choice nor by design on the part of a substantial number of Canadian women.

Molly Lamb Bobak, *Unidentified CWAC Reading*, ca. 1943.

ONE

Onward and Upward:

The Pre-Mobilization Years (1938–1941)

T HE UNPRECEDENTED CONTRIBUTION OF CANADIAN women during the First World War both at home and overseas was recognized in May 1918, when a subcommittee of the Militia Council in Ottawa was formed to consider the future establishment of a corps – to be known as "The Canadian Women's Corps."[1]

In principle, the council actually approved the formation of such a corps in September 1918; however, by then victory was at hand, and the Armistice brought an end to any further investigative forays in that direction.

In the United Kingdom, though, the idea died less gracefully.[2] The women's corps that had formed as auxiliaries to each of the three services in Britain had been disbanded after the war, but a nucleus of die-hards – many of them women who had belonged to one or another of these auxiliary corps – committed themselves to a persistent and persuasive campaign aimed at some form of female mobilization for the future. After all, it had been proved that women could be useful in many capacities – as clerks, typists, cooks, waitresses, maids, messengers, even drivers.

By 1934 there were hopeful indications that the efforts towards mobilization of women were being rewarded. The Women's Reserve Sub-committee of the Committee on Imperial Service was set up to examine the matter more closely, but after two years of intermittent meetings, the subcommittee came out against the idea. A peace-time women's corps seemed to serve no useful purpose at that point. For the moment, at least, any hope held out for involvement in the militia – even in an auxiliary capacity – was put aside, albeit briefly.

By 1937, the rise of Nazi Germany had become the source of great concern in Britain. The official position opposing the inclusion of a women's reserve corps was completely reversed, and a year later, in September 1938, royal assent had been given for the enlistment of 2,000 women between the ages of eighteen and fifty as volunteers into the Auxiliary Territorial Service (ATS). Each company was to be commanded by a female officer and was to be affiliated with a unit of the Territorial Army.

By April 1939 the British Admiralty had taken steps towards the formation of the Women's Royal Naval Service (WRNS), and three months later the Women's Auxiliary Air Force (WAAF) was granted official status. The wheels were in motion.

The official induction of these auxiliary militia corps also provided inspiration in Britain for the formation or revitalization of civilian volunteer organizations by the dozen: the First Aid Nursing Yeomanry (FANYS) of the First World War, the Women's Mechanized Transport Service, the Civilian Nursing Reserve, the Red Cross, the St. John Ambulance Brigade, the British Legion, and the Women's Volunteer Services for Civil Defence, to name but a few.

Any connection between the reversal of official policy in the U.K. and subsequent events in Canada is purely speculative, but it does appear to have had some effect, especially on those women in Canada whose political awareness was high or whose ties with England were strong. These were the first to feel the urge to mobilize themselves in some capacity to prepare for a war that, after the Munich crisis, appeared next to inevitable.

The first group in Canada to take any clear-cut action got off the ground in Victoria, B.C., early in October 1938, just a few weeks after royal assent had been granted for enlistment of women in the British ATS.

An original member of this Victoria B.C. Ancillary Corps recalls:

> There was much enthusiastic marching about and drill in the big armouries . . . It was obvious to all of us that there was going to be a war and we jolly well better start preparing for it – women as well as men! Our first meeting was held in a little upstairs place in the Hard of Hearing Hall. We

thought perhaps about twenty or so would show up, but to our amazement more than a hundred women appeared from nowhere.

We formed almost at once into four divisions: Motor Transport, Commissariat (supplies), Red Cross First Aid, and Clerical. We also decided on a uniform for ourselves; a white shirtwaist, blue skirt, blue sweater and a beret with a blue badge and the letters WVS (Women's Volunteer Service) in gold.

One of my functions as a volunteer was to drive for the Army's Military District (M.D.) Eleven. And my first experience, I can only describe as harrowing! It was quite a trick trying to manoeuvre a three-ton truck down one of Victoria's main streets on a Sunday morning. Thank heavens, it was Sunday! The vehicle was obviously never meant to be driven by a woman . . . certainly not one whose legs were so short that the brake pedal was barely in reach . . . and as for seeing out the rear window – totally impossible![3]

By the time thirteen other similar corps had formed in B.C., the need for a province-wide organization seemed obvious. The B.C. Women's Service Corps headed by Mrs. Norman Kennedy (later Lieut. Col. Joan B. Kennedy, CWAC) became the interim solution. Not unexpectedly, the corps patterned itself on the recently formed British ATS. But soon it became evident that for practicality's sake, if nothing else, an affiliation with the Red Cross might be a step in the right direction. The B.C. corps was subsequently disbanded and its members formed part of the Red Cross Volunteer Corps, which was also organized into diverse units similar to those of the B.C. Women's Service Corps.

Canada's declaration of war in September 1939 only served to accelerate the move toward female mobilization on a grander scale. The B.C. corps decided among themselves that a representative should be sent to Ottawa to lobby for official recognition of the corps as an army auxiliary similar to the British ATS. Perhaps to provide themselves with greater credibility, Mrs. Kennedy, accompanied by Mrs. Arthur Nation, made a six-week tour of the country to assess the status of other volunteer corps, which were also anxious to obtain some form of recognition: "Each of us anted up two dollars apiece and Joan Kennedy went off to Ottawa and talked to several politicians and so forth. They all appeared sympathetic

A brief was presented to the minister of defence, among others, but, for all its persuasiveness, it turned out to be "premature" in terms of national necessity.

The reasons behind this lack of active response – these kindly pats on the head, in essence – may have been obscure to those public-spirited women who were so busily forming local organizations, some paramilitary and others of a somewhat more domestic nature. Certainly at no time were the reasons for the rejection of military status for women ever made clear, and this, quite naturally, led to an even greater sense of frustration if not downright fury on the part of those women who wanted to assume a more active role in the war. Husbands, brothers, fathers, boyfriends were all joining up – doing something to help win the war. Surely women could help, as well!

By the time the final Order-in-Council (P.C.#4798) was passed in July 1941, giving birth to the Canadian Women's Auxiliary Air Force (CWAAF), between eighty and ninety organizations involving some 17,000 women across Canada had grown increasingly insistent in their demand for some form of official recognition. Besides the Red Cross, several of these self-designated corps had fashioned themselves after existing auxiliaries in Britain – complete with their own uniforms, ranking hierarchy, marching, drills, and in some cases even "musketry" training.

Nova Scotia and Alberta had each formed women's service corps. Then came the Women's Transport Service, a national organization, and in Quebec, a Women's Volunteer Reserve Corps. Saskatchewan had its own branch of the Auxiliary Territorial Service, and another national organization, the Canadian Auxiliary Territorial Service (CATS), soon emerged. Its marching song boasted a zealous passion to participate more actively in the war effort.

> We will fight for the might
> That we know is right
> And even Mussolini knows
> The CATS can fight! . . .[5]

In many instances the aims and objectives of these organizations were more patriotic than practical, and corps members with a realistic turn of mind probably realized that the enemy could very well be at the gates before Canada's women would be handed anything more threatening than a monkey wrench or a mop.

Meanwhile, the government was bombarded with never-ending pleas, petitions, demands, and supplications from these volunteer corps and associations. MPs, military "brass" and others in high places were continually badgered with letters, briefs, telegrams, phone calls and even, when possible, personal visits. Ottawa was under siege.

And from Britain came a personal letter to Air Vice-Marshal William (Billy) Bishop from the pen of Lady Rachel Stuart on behalf of the WAAF. Lady Stuart had spent a number of years in Canada and wished to express her great interest in the possibility of forming a Canadian women's auxiliary to the Air Force. Would her assistance in such an endeavour be useful in any way?

While Air Vice-Marshal Bishop was most likely impressed with Lady Stuart's good intentions and organizational skills, her offer of assistance was gracefully and graciously turned down.[6] Nearly two years later, when air and ground crews were desperately needed, six British WAAF officers were made available to implement Lady Stuart's original suggestion and were of invaluable assistance in the setting up of the Canadian Women's Auxiliary Air Force (later the RCAF WDs).

Perhaps as a result of the onslaught from both sides of the Atlantic, Ottawa sent out some faint, deceptively encouraging signs of response to requests for female mobilization. The associate deputy minister of war services had met with Senator Cairine Wilson and others to discuss the possibility of holding a nation-wide conference, a "mass meeting," which would include representatives from all the larger organizations of women volunteers. Its object would be the creation of a centralized volunteer bureau "on a national scale."[7]

On the other hand, there was absolutely no mention in all of this of voluntary military service for Canadian women. The potential usefulness of women in the militia – Canadian women, in any case – was still not accepted in military circles. The increasing impatience of women would simply have to go on being ignored because Canadian Military Headquarters (CMHQ) had no policy and seemed in no great hurry to develop one. Hell might well freeze over before any attention was given to the matter.

For one thing, certain high-ranking strategists were opposed to the whole concept of Canadian women being mobilized in the military sense. Should the situation overseas alter drastically, the idea might – possibly – be reconsidered.

In Britain, meanwhile, appeals had long since been launched to the four corners of the Commonwealth for women to serve in the volunteer branch of the ATS. In fact, Prime Minister Mackenzie King's personal correspondence included a request from Her Royal Highness Princess Alice, commander-in-chief of the volunteer ATS and wife of Canada's governor general. If permission were granted to recruit women in Canada, could special consideration (if not preference) be given to the ATS? The letter was forwarded to the minister of national defence (J.L. Ralston), with the suggestion that General Crerar, Canadian chief of general staff, and members of the Cabinet might discuss participation of Canadian women in the U.K.'s volunteer services. This was, however, deemed premature. Eventually they might be useful as military transport drivers of ambulance and staff cars for Canadian units, but General P.J. Montague had already advised, almost a year earlier, that "they (women) should be confined to very minor use."[8]

At CMHQ in London, however, there had been some "internal discussion" taking place.[9] The advantages of having a Canadian women's auxiliary force were becoming more apparent. Canadians on overseas duty in Britain were witnessing at first hand the effectiveness of Britain's mobilization of women. They were also much closer to the war. By the summer of 1940, France had capitulated and Dunkirk was behind them. The desperate need for increased manpower was coming in loud and clear. Female clerks, they decided, were more skilled and more readily available. Furthermore, they would cost less to employ. And, as everyone knew, Canadian women were more than willing to serve. The single disadvantage of such a plan appeared to be administrative. The inclusion of this new element in the militia would, of necessity, create additional complications.

In any case, for all its good intentions, with which the road to hell is so well paved, this particular proposal, for reasons unknown, never left England.

At CMHQ in Canada the formation of a women's corps was still "under discussion." No policy had emerged; nor had any answer been given to the pleas of women from one end of Canada to the other. Their level of frustration, according to one former women's service corps member, was coming close to the boiling point: "We were positively chafing at the bit, but all we got from Ottawa was little pats on the head . . . Just go home and keep knitting . . . In other words, 'Don't call us, we'll call you!'"[10]

Certainly the following excerpt from a letter to the Honourable J.T. Thorson, then minister of auxiliary war services, reflects the sense of urgency – almost to the point of desperation – which was shared by countless women's corps members across Canada. They wanted to play a direct part – to perform some active, useful function, and if it could be in the uniform of an officially recognized corps, so much the better!

> Here in Winnipeg, I have been organizing classes and drill for girls for the past eleven months, with the result that we (the Manitoba Women's Auxiliary Corps) have many girls who could fill the requirements of Lord Beaverbrook's appeal for women who will be trained as radio technicians in Britain. We are set up on a military basis, for the express purpose of assisting the armed forces, as the women of Britain are ... It would however be necessary to have Ottawa's approval, if not authority, for we must be certain that the Order-in-Council (P.C.# 2371) prohibiting Canadian women from entering the war zone would be lifted in this instance ... We are anxious to know what the regulations are in regard to Lord Beaverbrook's appeal. He obviously wants women from this side of the Atlantic, but are the girls to pay their own expenses and maintain themselves? Are certain educational qualifications necessary? We can easily recruit women, but we must know first, what will be expected of them.

The letter went on to request "a talk," since the writer was going to be in Ottawa for a few days and mentioned the minister's acquaintance with her husband, who was now on active service. Since they had no children, she was quite free to give her time to war work. She was also "willing and anxious to go overseas, if I can help there . . . After all, every one of us is needed in this war . . ." And at the bottom of the corps' official stationery the words "There'll always be an England" helped to emphasize her point.

And on Parliament Hill there were already a few converts to the cause. C.L. Church, MP for Broadview, strongly supported the idea of women in a more active role: "I believe that the women of Canada have a grievance ... They were given to believe last fall that their services would be utilized."[11]

Similar sentiments were expressed by MP John Diefenbaker, but it was all to no avail. The time might have come to talk of these things but it would be quite some time before talk gave way to action or any concrete plan.

Gradually, however, "discussions" at CMHQ began to take a more positive turn. Women employed in the militia as clerks might be just as suitable, if not more so, than male clerks, whose numbers were decreasing rapidly. Slowly, slowly, the advantages of granting military status to women started to outweigh the concomitant problems such a move would entail. Women in the militia could be controlled by the Department of National Defence (DND) as opposed to the civil service. They could be moved from one place to another as the need arose. The suggestion was put forward that they would take on "a military point of view," which would improve the standard of their work. And finally, they could "exhibit and realize their part in the war effort."[12]

The disadvantages of involving women were largely related to costs: the cost of outfitting them, of medical and dental service, and (not unexpectedly) the extra cost of providing them with special (and separate) accommodation.

Another objection to the presence of females in uniform was the spectre of favouritism. The problem of deciding which (if any) of the diverse volunteer groups should be officially recognized was simply too complicated. Perhaps, after all, the best solution to this endlessly tiresome dilemma would be to set up "an entirely new organization, which could not be the object of jealousy or competition among the voluntary groups."[13]

Adjutant-General Browne's remarks on the subject are illuminating:

> Owing to the jealous claims which will undoubtedly be put forward by these (volunteer) organizations if given recognition – it will not be possible to utilize these corps as such, either in whole or part. The establishment of an entirely NEW corps, with open recruiting, will be the only satisfactory method for some time to come.

But the idea of women in uniform was still strange to many people. For the hard-core "career soldier" types within the military it was a preposterous notion – a nightmare! How could a woman possibly adjust and submit to the discipline and rigours of life in the service? And many civilians, as well, found the idea of women in uniform entirely unsuitable, if not unthinkable. Military service was simply not an acceptable occupation for women – it could lead to all sorts of immoral behaviour. A woman's place was in the home and that was exactly where she should remain for the duration.

The wholesale acceptance of women in the military was little more than a distant dream. In effect, the consensus was that every able-bodied man should be employed before the use of womanpower was given any further thought. The status quo should be maintained at all costs! And the mindset that could not deal with the *idea* of women in uniform had an even harder time accepting the reality, once the die had been cast. The fact that these women were playing an active and essential part in a war that the Allies, even with their help, were desperately close to losing was apparently of little consequence to many Canadians, male and female alike.

During a visit to London in November 1940, however, the minister of defence held talks with Vincent Massey (the Canadian high commissioner) and General P.J. Montague. He came away with "the very strong impression" that *if* women were to be utilized to a greater extent, it would be preferable to have them administered as military personnel, by the services, rather than by the government as civilians employed by the Department of War Services. Three months later, Major-General Browne, the adjutant-general, made a recommendation to the minister of national defence that a "Canadian Women's (Army) Service be established." He was of the opinion that the time had come. "Women's services must now be utilized to a much greater extent than at present."

Politically, this solution to the manpower shortage was also a great deal more palatable than raising the issue of conscription before its time had come. If it was a question of choosing between the mobilization of women who had demonstrated their eagerness to become involved militarily and the enlistment selection of unwilling males, then, clearly, women were the safer bet.

The next step was to test the waters, to see how the idea would be received by the various services. Commanding officers were canvassed across Canada, and the reactions to the possibility of enlisting women registered everything from warm enthusiasm to outrage on a grand scale. One area commander argued that the obstacles in the path of such a drastic undertaking were insurmountable. The location of his station, for example, was completely inaccessible (for women) – even though it was only three and a half miles from a city and serviced by a paved road and a bus route.

On the other hand, there were others who were more clear-sighted and realized that somehow the manpower shortage had to be remedied, and if women were willing to "join up" why not make the most of it? There was, after all, a war on . . .

At a tri-service conference held in April 1941, this division of opinion persisted; however, those with mixed feelings and those strongly opposed to female mobilization outnumbered the more open-minded participants. The Navy was not yet convinced that there was sufficient need to warrant the integration of women into the Senior Service. The RCAF was "making plans" and the Army was waffling. There was still a surplus of "low category" men (those unfit for combat duty) whose services should be made use of before women were brought into the picture.

There was, however, unanimous agreement that if and when women were to be mobilized, each service would entirely control any auxiliary women's service that might be formed. In effect, if there was going to be recruitment, it should definitely *not* be left to the Department of National War Services to supply women to the forces. Direct recruitment by each service was the only possible route to follow. In the meantime, women should be employed in industry if necessary. The shortage of manpower, initially, was not as acute as the shortage of aircraft and munitions. Then, in May 1941, yet another report was published, this time to the effect that the Defence Department should come to some sort of decision. Would it be one auxiliary force administered by the Department of National War Services; or would each of the forces be responsible for its own separate "arm" or "wing"? Things were becoming more than a little embarrassing at this point, since there had been a request from the British Air Ministry for permission to send across a substantial number of British airwomen to work on British Commonwealth Air Training Stations. As well, the RAF was urging the immediate formation of a Canadian auxiliary force for women and indicated that Canadian airwomen would be welcomed on air stations in Great Britain, as well.

The proposal caused considerable consternation: how could all these British WAAFs be accommodated on RCAF stations? And how would Canadian members of the many women's para-military auxiliaries react to the sight of boatloads of uniformed WAAFs arriving on their doorstep? It was, as Lester B. Pearson pointed out in a letter to Vincent Massey, very awkward for the Canadian government to have British servicewomen in Canada, "while no provision has been made for the organization of corresponding services in this country."[14]

The British Air Ministry's unexpected proposal, in a sense, forced the hand of the Canadian government. It must come to a decision. "Zero hour," as one senior RCAF officer called the induction of women into the forces, was not as far off as certain individuals would have liked. Many men still blanched at the thought of women wearing the same uniform as they did – in fact, any uniform at all, unless it was a nurse's or a parlour maid's. It was an unnerving possibility!

At long last, the situation was brought to a head in June 1941, when the British Mechanized Transport Corps was granted permission to recruit women in Canada for overseas duty. This, in addition to the imminent arrival of several thousand WAAFs, called for immediate action. It was simply a matter of deciding who would do the recruiting. Would it be the War Services Department or the armed forces?

Each of the three services had already made it abundantly clear that it wished to do its own recruiting, thank you very much! But, by now, the National War Services Department had created a potential "pool" of women – a "manning pool" – whose personnel could be turned over for enlistment.

There were, however, certain disadvantages to using only women drawn from a pool of volunteer services. Many of these women were past the accepted age, many had physical impairments or medical problems and would not pass a fitness test, and many had had no practical training. Surely it would be better to have an open door (and mind?) and call upon women who were already holding down responsible jobs – women, in other words, who were not free to join volunteer auxiliaries. And in the same month as the permission came for Canadian women to enlist for overseas duty in Britain, a highly placed RCAF official serving in England wrote back to his confreres in Canada urging the formation of an RCAF women's division, using the British WAAF's success as his prime ammunition. They had released manpower for other work and raised the standard of efficiency, discipline and morale on RAF stations. Contrary to popular belief, accommodation had *not* been a problem, nor was "segregation" either necessary or desirable.

There was also a suggestion that, should a Canadian RCAF women's auxiliary force be formed, the first step must be the training of a select group of officers and NCOs, which could then form the nucleus from which the force would eventually develop.

A request for two WAAF officers to be sent to Canada was dispatched and an affirmative reply was received. They would be on the first available ship. As for recruiting, the general organization would come under the jurisdiction of the War Services Department, but the detailed organization would be worked out by each service – a perfect example of the Canadian fine art of compromise. And towards the end of June 1941 came the following press release from the DND Public Relations Office:

DEPARTMENT OF NATIONAL DEFENCE
PUBLIC RELATIONS OFFICE
(ARMY)

O T T A W A: June 27, 1941.
                                                              Release No. 734

It has been decided to establish a Women's Auxiliary Corps for the Army which will be known as the "CANADIAN WOMEN'S ARMY CORPS."

During the next six months it is estimated that from two to three thousand women can be absorbed into the Army to take over certain tasks now performed by soldiers thus relieving men for service in field formation overseas. These women will take over tasks such as:

Drivers of light Mechanical Transport vehicles.

Cooks in hospitals and messes.

Clerks, Typists and Stenographers at camps and training centres.

Telephone operators, and messengers.

Canteen helpers.

Storewomen.

Women joining the C.W.A.C. will be required to enrol under approximately the same conditions as for soldiers. They will be medically examined, documented, and clothed. They will be paid at rates somewhat lower than those authorized for soldiers and comparable with Civil Service rates. Women will be eligible for promotion up to the equivalent of Commissioned rank.

Women required for the Army will be selected from a register of women which is to be maintained by the Minister of National War Services. The procedure will be for Defence Headquarters, upon requesting women, to make its demands on the Minister of National War Services stating the number, type of employment and place required. When the women report they will, after a probationary period, be enrolled in the Canadian Women's Army Corps for service, and will then be administered entirely by the Department of National Defence.

As some time will elapse before uniforms and suitable accommodation can be made ready, the enrolment of women will be gradual and at first limited to places where they can be billeted.

The allowance granted to women who cannot be accommodated in quarters will be at the present Army rates.

In the event of uniforms not being available when a woman enrols, she will be given a working dress or other distinguishing mark to show that she is serving with the Army, or, if in possession of a uniform of her previous Corps, will be permitted to wear it until her Canadian Women's Army Corps uniform is issued.

It is proposed to appoint a senior officer of the Canadian Women's Army Corps at Defence Headquarters to co-operate with the staff in dealing with Women's services in the Army.

Two months after the army's press release, the Royal Canadian Air Force issued its official call to arms.

ROYAL CANADIAN AIR FORCE

Enlistment of women in the various trades will be commenced shortly and the first course of training will begin at the C.W.A.A.F. Training Depot in the Old Havergal College at Toronto early in December. There are nine trades from which a prospective C.W.A.A.F. recruit may select the one for which she feels most suited. These are: administrative; clerks, general and stenographic; cooks; transport drivers; equipment assistants; fabric workers; hospital assistants; telephone operators; and standard duties which includes general duty and mess women.

The two travelling selection boards which commenced this work to hold coast-to-coast sittings have discovered a keen interest among Canadian women in this new organization which is affiliated officially with the Royal Canadian Air Force. Sittings have already been held in Ottawa and are continuing this week in Montreal and Toronto. During the next ten days 150 applicants will be selected for a five-weeks' instructional course. The first officers and N.C.O.'s will be chosen from among those making the best showing in each group. Subsequent courses will be of four week's duration.

Besides instruction, the course at Toronto will provide certain periods each day for drill and physical training, with the remainder of time devoted to lectures and practical work in the designated trades.

Press Release C.W.A.A.F. –
RCAF – Sept. 20, 1941

Molly Lamb Bobak, *CWAC Sitting on a Bench*, ca. 1943.

TWO

Joining Up

WHILE THE CANADIAN ARMY'S DECISION to enlist women was almost simultaneous with that of the RCAF, the Air Force was the first to receive official sanction. The Order-in-Council (P.C. #4798) granting the RCAF permission to enlist women into what would be known initially as the Canadian Women's Auxiliary Air Force was passed on July 2, 1941, a matter of weeks before the Army received the go-ahead on August 13, 1941 (Order-in-Council P.C. #6289). Both services, however, began the actual process of enlistment at about the same time in the early autumn.

The Navy, on the other hand, continued to reserve judgment on the question of female enlistment, preferring perhaps to observe the experience from the bridge for a while, with no apparent concern over the possibility that the other two forces might have skimmed off the cream by the time it opted to recruit women – if indeed such a time ever came. Parliament approved formation of the Women's Royal Canadian Naval Service (the "Wrens") on July 31, 1942 (Order-in-Council P.C. #56-6775), almost a year after the competition had begun recruiting.

In comparison to several other dominions within the British Empire, Canada was one of the last off the starting block. Auxiliary forces for women had been formed in South Africa (November 1939), New Zealand (February 1941), and Australia (March 1941).[1]

Canadian Forces Photographic Unit, DND, PL-17900

A tri-service gathering, Ottawa, Ont. (ca. 1943)

In Russia, women had long since come under fire. The valour of Soviet women in combat has been well documented. Valerie Khomyakova, the Flying Witch, became the first woman to destroy an enemy aircraft at night. Later in the war, she was killed in action along with a number of her comrades in the 586th Women's Aircraft Fighter Squadron, the 46th Night Bomber Squadron and the 125th Squadron for Daylight Bombing. Women also served with distinction as tank crew members, machine gunners, snipers and in artillery units. In addition one of every ten Partisan fighters was a woman.[2]

It can be argued with some legitimacy that had Canadian women come under direct attack under similar circumstances, they would have acquitted themselves equally well. Fortunately this was never put to the test.

In any event, the traditions associated with each of the three branches of Canada's armed services at the time were also reflected in the organization and operation of the women's services. Each in turn established its own ground rules and fiercely asserted its separate identity right from the start. To the casual civilian observer these distinctions may have been limited to the most obvious: the distinctive uniforms worn by the members of each of the three services. There were, of course, a great many other, subtler, differences, which could only be determined at closer range.

Initially, both the Canadian Women's Army Corps (CWAC) and the Canadian Women's Auxiliary Air Force (CWAAF) were set up as separate entities, under the aegis of the Army and the Air Force respectively but nonetheless operating as auxiliaries or components rather than as integral parts of the affiliate service. This, too, eventually changed.

Unidentified recruit being sworn into the CWAC in the presence of two army officers.

In February 1942, after much deliberation, the Air Force announced its decision to alter the status of the CWAAF and create the Women's Division of the RCAF. The Army followed suit in March 1942; the CWAC's separate status had led to increasing difficulties. The problems of control, supervision, administration, and benefits were creating unnecessary headaches, which might well be alleviated by a change in status.

The Women's Royal Canadian Naval Service (WRCNS or Wrens) on the other hand, was officially considered as part of the Navy from the beginning, and thus avoided some of the difficulties encountered by the other two services. In actual fact, because there were virtually no Canadian women with naval experience, the Royal Canadian Navy (RCN) relied heavily upon the advice of several British Women's Royal Naval Service officers who had been asked to help out with the organization of the Canadian counterpart. As a result the WRCNS tended to be a separate, if not auxiliary, force at the outset and it was only by degrees that it was gradually absorbed into the general scheme of things.

Whatever their original difficulties may have been in terms of status, all three services were faced with more or less similar problems when it came to recruitment. Each wanted to establish its identity and reputation by attracting high-calibre recruits to fill enlistment quotas. There is some evidence that the WRCNS was the most successful. It was a substantially smaller force (with a total enlistment of under 7,000, compared to the CWAC with over 22,000 on its roster, and the Air Force WD's 17,000 plus) and it seems to have encountered the least difficulty with both the selection of personnel and general *esprit de corps*. Possibly, too, the fact that the Navy only reached the decision to recruit women almost a year later than the other two services contributed to this. Having profited by observation, the Navy sailed on smoother waters.

Third Officer McQueen (right) and WRCNS recruiting staff, Vancouver, B.C., April 16, 1943.

The problem of attracting and enlisting "suitable types" as volunteers was certainly common to all three women's services, although each service attempted to solve it in a slightly different way. There is no question that the decision on the part of the Air Force, and later the Navy, to rely on the experience of British WAAF and WRNS officers paid certain dividends. The Army, on the other hand, preferred to rely on its own personnel and the experience of the hundreds of Canadian women who had been members of the host of officially unrecognized auxiliary corps prior to the creation of the CWAC.

Still, the practical aspects of mounting a recruitment campaign were essentially the same, whether it was the Army, the Navy, or the Air Force. Each service had to come up with the best possible enticements – appealing to patriotism and to women's sense of duty, seeking out those women who wanted to do more . . . "to free a man to fight" . . . "to serve that men might fly." These exhortations rolled off the presses and over the airwaves, and there was no shortage of women willing to answer the call – from farm girls to debutantes. From factories, universities, department stores, offices, and classrooms, women flocked to the recruiting centres set up across the country. Eventually mobile units were created in order to obtain maximum accessibility, but originally recruiting centres were confined to larger cities and towns, and there was no shortage of willing applicants.

In an official RCAF bulletin issued June 30, 1942, the criteria for enlistment were clearly defined:

Airwomen enlist as R.C.A.F. personnel do; at recruiting centres throughout Canada, at each of which an officer of the Women's Division is posted, and provision made for special staff and medical examination rooms.

To be eligible for enlistment an applicant must :
1. Have attained her 18th birthday and not have attained her 41st birthday.
2. Have a medical category A4B or higher (equivalent to Army Standard A).
3. Be five feet or over in height and conform to the required weight standard.
4. Have a minimum education standard of High School Entrance.
5. Be able to pass the appropriate trade test.
6. Be of good character with no record of conviction for an indictable offence.

DND-12223

RCAF (WD) class at #1 Rockcliffe Basic Training, April 1942.

Applicants will not be considered for enlistment:
1. If they hold permanent Civil Service appointments.
2. If they are married women who have children dependent on them for care and upbringing (i.e., sons under 16 and daughters under 18).

The selection process for potential servicewomen was not without its complications, however. The need to develop recruiting techniques that would make it possible to reject "some of the chaff that comes in with the wheat" soon became abundantly clear. And even the question of which was wheat and which was chaff was a matter of concern to officers charged with the responsibility of accepting or rejecting candidates who presented themselves for enlistment.

A CWAC officer in Toronto fired off this query to her superiors regarding the application of a girl of "Indian nationality" who was at the top of her class in a draughting course at Central Technical School: "Please advise whether a member of this race would be objected to for enlistment in the Corps." The reply: no objections whatsoever.

Those placed in charge of mobile recruiting units in more isolated communities appear to have had a particularly difficult time of it. In Geraldton in Northern Ontario, there was the problem of "complacency." According to the recruiting officer assigned to the area, the town was "full of miners" and in general the populace was "not receptive." It seems the search for girls who were both "serious-minded and sensible" was not for the faint of heart. Another report noted that it was difficult to persuade girls to leave the farm when their brothers were still in evidence. In Fannysteele, Ontario, a poor response was attributed to "foreigners and habitual French speech . . . the mixture of French, Ukrainian and Polish is not conducive to recruiting."

In Mooshorn, a checkup on manpower and the actions of the local citizenry was recommended. There were "quite a number of people of German descent and on some occasions there has been bad feeling between the different nationalities." In another community the report came back that there were "quite a few girls of foreign extract [sic]. It seems to be against their principles to join the forces."

There was also concern expressed after a visit to a certain district that was "well populated with zombies and dodgers who appear to be quite proud of the fact that they have so far hoodwinked the authorities . . . A machine gun would be the only method of persuasion here."

And in another Northern town a dance was held for the express purpose of attracting prospective recruits. The results were evidently not what had been anticipated by the organizer. "The dance was well attended by white people but the presence of the Indians seated around the edge seemed to slow it up at times."

On the other hand, at another stop along the route no dance was held, as the dancehall was owned by "a Frenchman who refused to rent it to us." And in a number of instances where halls were made available, it was observed that the "motley" audience who had come to see the recruitment show was "well primed – liquidly."

Fortunately there were a few places where the local hall was filled to capacity and "attended by old and young with enthusiasm and a fine patriotic spirit displayed."

And a report from Fort Frances included information on a certain questionable volunteer. "This girl is an American who wanted to enlist but I was suspicious of her, so checked up with the American immigration and found out she had a bad character and a police record. She may try to enlist again for she had good qualifications and education. Please copy name for future reference."[3]

It was also necessary for those involved in the recruitment process to spot any applicant who might be regarded as unsatisfactory "because of inferior intelligence or personality traits suggestive of psychiatric disabilities. The applicant will be referred to a psychiatrist and if considered unsuitable for employment in the CWAC he (the psychiatrist) will refer her to the Medical Board for rejection on medical grounds." The complexities of selecting suitable recruits clearly required great perception and perseverance.

The Pacific Command recruiting officer of the CWAC wrote a letter on March 10, 1943, bemoaning the lack of public support for the recruitment of women:

There has not been created, even after three years of war, a general public opinion that women are needed in the Army. Just how folks could be blasted from their complacency is difficult to know . . . Recruiting staffs are fighting valiantly to instill the great seriousness of this war.

A true conception of the situation has not yet really permeated the hearts and breasts of the general public . . . There are still many soldiers who resent women in the Forces. Many others do not encourage enlistment. It is difficult to break this down.

A letter to the minister of war services, the Hon. J.T. Thorson, raised another question:

The Secretary,   November 25, 1941
Dept. of National Defence for Air,
Ottawa, Ontario

Enlistment – Cooks – C.W.A.F.
1.   Further to your above referred letter, may it be respectfully suggested that particular care be given, so that C.W.A.F. candidates, from this District, have a sufficient knowledge of English, for their trade, before being asked to report to this Recruiting Centre for enlistment.
2.   To illustrate this point, there was a Miss (unnamed) from Tourelle, Gaspé Co., P.Q., who reported, under orders, to this Recruiting Centre, 24-11-41, for enlistment as "Cook." This lady has experience, fine appearance, good education, and has passed her medical examination with flying colours. Unfortunately, she cannot understand or speak a word of English, and, we will be obliged to send her back home without being enlisted. As it is

Guests at Tri-Service Garden Party hosted in their honour at Queen's Park by Ontario Lt.-Governor Albert Matthews, September 11, 1943.

considered that it would not be in the best interest of the Service, under the present circumstances, to tell her the reason she cannot be enlisted, we will have to tell her a long story, so as to keep her happy and prevent criticism, until such time as we will be able to proceed with her enlistment.

3. As the language question is a battle horse for criticism in this District, may it be permitted once more, to suggest that particular care be taken so that only bilingual applicants be advised to report for C.W.A.A.F. enlistment at this Recruiting Centre.

4. It is not the intention of this Recruiting Centre to criticize the methods used by A.F.H.Q., but to respectfully draw their attention to a very delicate and touchy subject. It is hoped that this letter will be taken in the spirit in which it is written, that is: That the best interests of the R.C.A.F. will be served.

Commanding Officer,
No. 14 Recruiting Centre
R.C.A.F., Quebec, P.Q.

The enlistment of servicewomen in the province of Quebec posed specific problems, not because of lack of willing recruits, but rather due to inadequate training facilities for volunteers who spoke only French. Until mid-1942, it had been necessary to reject all French Canadian candidates who were not bilingual because it was considered impossible for them to "absorb instruction."[4] This situation was remedied as each of the services set up its own School of English for francophone recruits.

The concerns of certain Quebec politicians over the potential difficulties French-speaking recruits might encounter are reflected in the following memo to the authorities in Ottawa:

In our country, as in all countries at war, women are called upon to bear a more and more active part in the service of victory. We know that the army will have its feminine units in Quebec City in a few weeks. A question comes naturally from the start: What treatment will French-Canadian women receive? Who will the officers be?

Evidently the Commanding Officer should be a French-Canadian woman, if the militia is to get the sympathy it needs. Errors committed in other fields should not be repeated by those who forget always the very great susceptibility of the French-Canadian population.

In the case of the feminine army, nobody will be permitted to claim or to allot all the posts to English-speaking ladies, that the military training of these is more advanced. Since this is a new start, all women have the same training . . . or rather, none are better prepared than others.[5]

No doubt, certain of these fears were allayed by the appointment of Madeleine St. Laurent (CWAC), an officer and a gentlewoman, who encouraged other French Canadian women to follow her example and actively take part in the march towards victory . . .

Now, we, as women, have obtained the right to participate in public affairs through our vote. Today we are taking yet another step forward and are asking our fathers, our husbands and our brothers to let us stand beside them in defence of our country and our liberty. In this way we can legitimately do our part in the struggle until the day of victory comes.

La Presse, January 17, 1942
(author's translation)

The powers that be have maintained that although women are taking an active part in the march towards victory . . . they will not be expected to bear arms – "a task reserved for the male sex." However, Jean Knox, director of the British ATS, maintains that this male exclusivity is based solely on such qualities as "virility," physical strength or courage . . . "I do not believe," she says, "that women are capable of taking lives to the degree that men are. Women are the givers of life. Even in an all-out war, women do not have the capacity to kill."

La Presse, September 30, 1942
(author's translation)

Nonetheless, there were many young women in Quebec, as well as elsewhere, whose sentiments could only be described as bellicose. In recalling her reactions to the war, a former servicewoman from *la belle province* appears to be among their number:

I devoured all the newspaper reports. For me the declaration of the war was comparable to the loss of someone close to me. The word frightened me in the same way as the words fire or famine. Canada must be defended. The Germans must be held off. At that moment I would love to have been able to personally attack Hitler. You heard a lot about espionage and I pictured myself as a spy on a mission to assassinate Hitler (not that I could have harmed a flea) . . . I could hardly wait for my eighteenth birthday. I wanted so badly to do something.

De la poêle à frire à la ligne de feu[6]
(Out of the Frying Pan and into the Firing Line)

Many French Canadian women had to contend with personal agonies and aggravation during their immersion in an English-speaking milieu. One former servicewoman recalls the experience of meeting a young girl from the Quebec City region who was on the same train to RCAF Basic Training camp at Rockcliffe. During the course of their journey they agreed that it would be a good idea to stick together, but on arrival they were immediately separated and told, "How do you expect to learn English that way?"

Another, a former CWAC trainee, remembers being sent to the School of English in Kitchener. It was traditional that at the end of the course the participants were to put on a series of skits and provide entertainment for their English-speaking compatriots. One group, with a certain degree of malice aforethought, presented their number – a popular First World War song, in French – having substituted their own words:

> Vous n'aurez pas les petites Canadiennes
> Et malgré vous, nous resterons françaises
> Vous avez pu angleçiser la plaine
> Mais notre coeur, vous ne l'aurez jamais . . .

Translated into English, it could have brought down more than the house:

> You won't ever get these little French Canadian girls
> We'll stay French, no matter what you do
> You might have made us English on the outside
> But our hearts will never be won over . . .

The audience remained oblivious to the song's implications, and since it was all very rhythmical and moving, everyone cheered and clapped enthusiastically – with one exception: a French-speaking officer who glared at the performers for the rest of the evening.[7]

An extravaganza called "You're in the Army Now" was presented at one point during a recruitment drive. The audience at the Montreal Forum was treated, as part of the entertainment, to a skit on female recruits being put through their paces by a male drill instructor. Every imaginable stereotype was depicted: the coquette, the scatterbrain, the food addict, the cry-baby, the whiner – the full gamut; and, of course, when instructed to turn right, the entire group turned left. The finale, however, set things straight and demonstrated how all these misfits and ingénues were miraculously transformed into exemplary soldiers in short order.

Then in early 1943 a nation-wide "whispering campaign" began to take its toll on female recruitment in general and the Army in particular. Three separate surveys were undertaken. Two internal inquiries were conducted by the CWAC[8] and the Air Force WD, and a third – a public opinion survey – was mounted by the Advertising Agencies of Canada and the Joint Committee on Combined Recruiting Promotion (Women's Services of the Three Armed Forces), entitled "An Enquiry into the Attitude of the Canadian Civilian Public towards the Women's Armed

Forces."[9] All three surveys indicated the need for change from within, but as well, it was clear that the whispering campaign reflected the opinions of a substantial number of Canadians, civilians and militia men alike. Public acceptance of the concept of women as part of the Canadian military was anything but universal, and unless immediate remedial action was taken, the effect on recruitment of women into the forces might be drastic. What self-respecting Canadian family would want its daughters and sisters associating with "camp followers" and other assorted "trash"?[10]

The attitude of family and friends was heavily weighted with disapproval towards female enlistment. Roughly 50 percent were not in favour – between 20 percent and 30 percent were indifferent. Those in the forces were 48 percent in favour; in civilian life, only 28 percent. Of the fathers surveyed, 27 percent approved; of the mothers, 21 percent. Of the boyfriends, those in the forces were only 25 percent in favour. Servicemen were, in essence, one of the major sources of the campaign against women in uniform. Women could work in factories with impunity, it seems, but they donned a uniform at their own risk. This appears to be borne out by an airwoman's written response to the authorities in charge of recruitment:

It might interest you to know that the men of the RCAF discourage a great many girls from joining the W.D. I would probably have been in uniform long ago if I had not been associating with airmen who do not approve of the W.D. Many of my friends cannot make up their minds and I think it is the airmen who are holding them back. One of my girlfriends was informed by an airman that he would not speak to her if she joined the W.D. It might be a good idea to teach the RCAF that girls in the W.D. are okay.[11]

"Malicious propaganda, gossip and careless talk,"[12] as one senior RCAF officer described the invective directed towards women in a military role, must be combated. His advice was to the effect that such misinformation could not be ignored and should be treated seriously by the authorities. He also suggested that rather than refuting such statements, the original source should be sniffed out, and offenders severely dealt with.

It was apparent that the effects of the virulent and pervasive whispering campaign could not be ignored. Steps must be taken, and quickly, to repair the damage and at the same time to entice women into uniform.

To this end two films were churned out courtesy of the National Film Board. *Proudly She Marches* and *Wings on Her Shoulders*, both narrated primarily by a male voice, made much of the fact that a young woman who enlisted in the service was not necessarily joining the ranks of the unfeminine, even if it was a redefined brand of femininity that was being presented.

Just how effective these two films were is anyone's guess, but in all probability they did help to persuade a few more women to take the plunge. In fact, according to the two films, it all looked rather fun – an amusing sort of game, where you had to play by the rules – but clearly nothing too serious was involved, and certainly there was no question of physical danger.

When viewed in the light of current thought on women's issues, these films take on a highly patronizing tone that would undoubtedly raise more than the consciousness of most feminists today. In all fairness, it must be remembered that these films were created for a specific purpose – to help the war effort – and designed for an audience that was likely to be receptive to the message intended.

A direct result of the female enlistment shortfall was a change in the pay scale in June 1943. Originally set at two-thirds of a man's pay, in accordance with the British example, the pay scale was elevated to four-fifths as an inducement to new recruits with patriotism in their hearts and money on their minds. Certainly there was never any concrete reason for this disparity in terms of performance on the job, or any scientific proof that women were 20 to 30 percent less effective or proficient than men. This discrepancy in pay persisted throughout the war and was never explained to the vast majority of servicewomen, who felt they were executing their duties as well if not better than their male counterparts.

Air Minister C.G. (Chubby) Power, speaking in the House of Commons on June 3, 1943, on the subject of pay and allowances for airwomen, stated that the original rate of pay for women in the armed forces was laid down in Britain early in the war, when surveys showed that three women would be required to replace every two men in uniform. In the light of recent information, however, it was found that women in the services had increased in efficiency to the point where five women effectively replaced four men.

Accordingly, the RCAF raised its rates of pay for women to a four-fifths ratio, with the exception of women doctors, who entered the service

Canadian Forces Photographic Unit, DND, PL-6914

Assistant Section Officer Frances Douglas and Military Transport driver J.M.K. Gausden of Montreal pose with visiting British screen star Greer Garson at Uplands Air Station, Ottawa, 1942.

as medical officers and as such received full rates of pay. Daily rates of pay for enlisted women now ranged from 90 cents for an airwoman second class, at the bottom of the pay scale, to $3.30 for the highest-ranking non-commissioned officer (NCO). Officers' pay began at $2.85, while a wing officer, at the top end of the scale, received $6.70.

But whether it was two-thirds or four-fifths the rate of a man's pay, money was not the deciding factor for most women who enlisted. Patriotism, the urge to participate more actively in the war effort, a spirit of adventure, even the opportunity of getting away from home were all much more closely related to individual women's motivation to join up. The fact that most of them had absolutely no conception of what they were getting themselves into would only become apparent to them once they found themselves in uniform with virtually no way out. Aside from recourse to motherhood, they were in "for the duration."

Before being offered the opportunity to serve her country, each potential servicewoman was obliged to provide the recruiting office with a doctor's certificate attesting to her state of health. Then, upon reporting to the unit or recruiting centre, she was once again medically examined prior to enrolment.

Here again, there were unforeseen complications, such as the experience of the registrar for the Department of National War Services in Halifax, who was clearly under stress when he wrote to Ottawa:

Since Monday of last week I have had Army officers and women continually telephoning or calling at this office for information and instructions. The climax came on Thursday afternoon when I received a large group by appointment. These women had been rejected by the Medical Board for trifling reasons, although all had been placed in Category "A" by their family physician at home. They had given up good positions and said good-bye to their families and friends. One had received a parting gift from her employer. I discovered that a number had been rejected because they were a few pounds out from the standards of weight and height laid down. I telephoned the hospital where the examinations had been made and asked them to check their scales. All scales in that institution weighed differently and on this plea, I was able to obtain a new Board.

October 7, 1941
Halifax

It seems, as well, that not every "physical" was conducted under ideal conditions, once wholesale recruitment got under way. In a letter to Army headquarters, the following suggestions were put forward for immediate implementation:

1. It is requested that particular attention will be given to all aspects of propriety when any C.W.A.C. personnel are being medically examined. That is, examination will only be conducted in a private room or screened portion of a ward with draped or curtained windows. In every instance it will be necessary that a nurse or female attendant is present.
2. These examinations, for food handlers in particular, will include inspection of the mouth, throat, hands, arms and axille end, also the neck and head for general body cleanliness and freedom from infectious skin lesions. Examination of the trunk and lower body will not be carried out unless for some particular medical indication when proper examining room draping of the patient will be looked after.

3. Criticism has reached this office from various sources as to lack of reasonable care in attending to the propriety of examination of females and it is requested that particular attention will be given to the above-noted suggestions in order to obviate any repetition of criticism, please.

Military District No.2 H.Q.

May 19, 1943   Toronto

Obviously, even the process of selection at the level of physical fitness occasionally provided evidence of human frailty on the part of examining physicians. But once a recruit had been found medically fit for service, having survived "the physical," she was on her way to greater glory: four to six weeks of Basic Training and a whole new world . . . in uniform!

Notebook

DEPARTMENT OF NATIONAL WAR SERVICES, CANADA

To be able to serve your country at this hour is an honour of which to be proud. This honour carries with it many responsibilities. Soldiering is not a glamorous job. Nearly always it means personal sacrifice.

In completing the enclosed application form, you are taking the first step to join the ranks of Canada's fighting services. The acceptance of women as full-time auxiliaries in the Armed Forces has given the women of Canada a real opportunity to serve, and at the same time enables the Defence Department to release men for Active Service where most needed.

(August 1941, "Information for the use of women who wish to apply for enrolment as full-time auxiliaries in the Canadian Armed Forces.")

Something completely new

I didn't join up for patriotic reasons at all. I was bored with teaching and had just broken up with someone I'd been going with for a long time so it seemed like a good idea to try something completely new. But I certainly had no idea, at the time, what I was letting myself in for . . . Most of the recruits who were joining up with me were a lot younger. I was twenty-nine already, and the recruiting officer said to me, "You may not like it, you know. Why don't you think it over for a while." But I had already made up my mind by then, so I just went ahead and did it.

Former officer, CWAC

A real eager beaver

There is no doubt in my mind that patriotism was my main motive for joining the army. My girlfriend and I joined up together. I was eighteen at the time and a real eager beaver. I had already been working in a munitions plant, but I decided that wasn't enough, even though my mother was dead set against it. She never told me exactly what her objections were. She was just against the whole idea and so was my uncle. But I went ahead and did it anyway, because I thought it was important.

Former member, CWAC

On the dotted line

The funny thing is that I don't really know why I ever enlisted in the first place. I never even questioned what I was doing. I simply went and signed my name on the dotted line. Now, it all seems a bit absurd and ridiculous to have given up university and a career for four years of sitting around an air station on the Prairies.

Former officer, RCAF (WD)

Can you type?

They always asked you if you could type . . . first off; and we all said no. Then you did an aptitude test; and then you were sent off for Basic Training. From there I went into what they called clerk-ops and it was a good thing, too, because they needed us overseas. Otherwise I might have been stuck on the Prairies somewhere.

Former member, RCAF (WD)

I could hardly wait to be old enough

Patriotism was a factor with a lot of people who joined up; but there were plenty of other reasons as well. A lot of people just wanted a change, just to get away from whatever it was that they were doing . . . As for me, I had a lot of male friends in the forces – fellows who were being killed right, left, and centre and I could hardly wait to be old enough to get into uniform myself. Initially, I applied to the Navy, but their age restrictions were different, so then I applied to the RCAF and they took me. Little did I think I'd end up in the wilds of Newfoundland for a year and a half.

Former member, RCAF (WD)

National Archives of Canada, PA-128211

Personnel of CWAC taking part in a Victory Loan display at the Capital Theatre, Ottawa, October 23, 1942.

It seemed like a good idea at the time

I joined up in Toronto. I'd been doing canteen work and in the summer I worked on a farm because they were screaming for girls to help out. Well, finally I decided when they started enlisting women that I might as well get into the service. A lot of my friends were going in, for one thing. I know I wasn't a flag waver – "King and Country" or any of that stuff. It just seemed to be a good idea at the time.

Former member, RCAF (WD)

I did it all on my own

When I signed up, I did it all on my own, didn't know a living soul when I got to Kitchener, where we did our Basic. For a while, too, I was scared to death they'd find out my age (I was sixteen), but that didn't last long because I found out there was a fourteen-year-old kid there. After that I felt brave.

Later on, towards the end, there was a party at the officers' mess and they sent me out to find a bottle. After I'd delivered it back, they asked me in for a drink and the major said to me, "You're still young, aren't you? When is it you turn twenty-one?" She had a straight face, maybe a little twinkle in her eye, but I knew right then and there that I hadn't really been fooling anybody. She'd known about my age all along.

Former member, CWAC

Slept with her teddy bear

They took a lot of kids in who were too young, really . . . Not that they didn't grow up in a heck of a hurry, but it wasn't easy on them. An awful lot of them couldn't cope with it. They'd go out and get full of beer and then come back and be sick and we'd have to clean them up and put them to bed. They didn't have the maturity . . . and a lot of them had never been more than fifty miles from home. I remember one of these youngsters slept with her teddy bear.

Former member, CWAC

Fast friends

A lot of women I served with had lost a husband or a brother or a boyfriend and that was their main reason for being there. Two in particular I remember – who normally would have nothing in common if they'd been civilians – but they became fast friends because of this common bond of having been widowed.

Former member, WRCNS

I liked the uniform best

I had a better chance of getting into the CWAC at an earlier age. I was sixteen. I think I liked the uniform best too.

Out West most of the posters were Army posters. I'm not sure why but there's no doubt about it, the posters did have some influence on me. Everywhere you looked, there were Army posters.

Former member, CWAC

We were willing to do anything
My girlfriend and I had both gone to the Army recruiting office when we were seventeen, because we had heard that they were taking seventeen-year-olds . . . and we begged them to take us. We were willing to do anything, but the ruling had not been changed. At least, that's what they told us. For one thing it was better than a regular job, or so we thought, and we'd be part of a group . . . And besides we really did feel that we were needed. The recruiting posters did a good job on that score, so as soon as I was old enough, I went right off to do my duty.

Former member, CWAC

A natural thing to do
After ten years of teaching, anything looked good. I think it was the idea of a change that attracted me as much as anything. And then too, all the men were going off and the uniforms had a certain attraction too. They really did look wonderful. And of course, a great number of us had been in this volunteer service corps, so once the Army started to enlist women, it seemed like the natural thing to do. Another reason why I chose the Army was that my fiancé had already joined.

Former member, CWAC

Looking for a change
I had a job, I was working but I was looking for a change. I didn't want to go to school and then one day I just said to myself, "The Army sounds good," and I liked the uniform . . . so that was that. And I think part of it was, too, that I had a lot of uncles that had joined up and fellows who were ahead of me at school; and it just seemed like the right thing to do. And, to tell you the truth, I've never regretted it. Character-wise it did a lot for me. It grew me up.

Former member, CWAC

Society girls
There were all sorts of official-looking people running around in what we called civilian uniforms. Most everyone who joined at the first had been in some kind of voluntary corps. Some of them were what you'd call society girls – lots of time and plenty of spending money – and so there was a bit of snobbery there. Those of us who came from the boonies, we really looked up to these women who were more or less designated as officers.

They had to have a nucleus of officers to begin with, and they had to find them somewhere, so it seemed logical, I guess, to draw from the top drawer, so to speak.

Former officer, CWAC

I didn't know one damn thing

The district officer commanding in Military District 2 was a personal friend, and when it came up that the Army was going to start taking in women, he called me down to his office and told me that they needed me. Because of all my experience down at the active service canteen, it seemed logical that I could be useful in the commissariat, which handles all the food. But he was more interested in finding a couple of top people to head up the recruiting. So there I was in the thick of it before I knew it. Of course, I didn't know one damn thing about marching and drill, and all that sort of thing. But we all learned soon enough. I became the company commander and had to lead the parades down to the armouries and prepare them for reviews, and the whole business. It was awful.

Furthermore, I didn't know anything about writing military letters and files and memos. Fortunately, I had a good assistant, a man who knew what it was all about. We sat for about six weeks in a pokey little office down on Adelaide Street – just two of us. The advertisement went out and we had to find four officers to start with and then try to screen the people who presented themselves to us as volunteers. Finally we got a company together, but it wasn't easy, because basically all we had to rely on was our intuition and common sense.

Former company commander, CWAC

I thought the uniform was beautiful

I had heard that it was a little more difficult to get into the Navy and I thought the uniform was beautiful . . . Whenever you saw "Wrens" out on the street, they always looked so smart. And you had to have really good references or they wouldn't look at you. They got the cream of the crop.

Former member, WRCNS

It certainly didn't appeal to me

Funny, the different things that influenced you one way or another. In my case, a friend of mine had joined the CWACs and was at the barracks in

WRCNS Recruiting Officer Nancy Pypher, 1943.

Old Trinity College over at St. George and Hoskin (in Toronto). The terrible tales she told about some of the intake in the ranks . . . about people having to be deloused and forcibly put in baths and things like that. It certainly didn't appeal to me, I can tell you. It made me think twice about the CWACs, believe me.

Former member, RCAF (WD)

Chosen regardless of their background

The application forms of 140 out of the 150 which are here at (CWAAF) Headquarters have been scrutinized, and

(1) Six of the girls who applied mentioned that they belonged to the Junior League.

(2) The occupations of the girls before joining were as follows:

Dietitians	8
Clerks, Stenos, etc.	60
P.T. Instructors	7
Laboratory Assts.	2
Librarians	5
Barristers	1
Nurses	3
Teachers	25
Social Workers	6
Saleswomen	1
Hospital Work	1
Own Business	2
Furrier	1
Dancer	1
Doctor's Assts.	1
No specified occupation	15

Of these latter 15; one was adjutant of the Canadian Women's Territorial Service; six were doing Red Cross work; one was married and at home; one has just left college; one was a pilot, and also doing Red Cross and social work. Three were specially interested in Girl Guides and camping; one has done social service work in hospital, and one has done social service work in connection with the I.O.D.E.

A general analysis of their voluntary activities shows that 57 belonged to the Red Cross, 32 to voluntary war services, 21 were Guides, 7 were camp controllers or commandants, 8 worked with the I.O.D.E., 9 did social work of different kinds and 5 worked with the C.G.I.T.

The points naturally most looked for by the Board were leadership and a sense of responsibility. Those girls who had given much of their time before or during the war to voluntary work of value to their country seemed to have developed both, and they were chosen regardless of their background.

Future promotions will depend entirely on the girls themselves and the impression they create in the work they do in the Stations.

H. Edwards
Air Vice-Marshal
for Chief of the Air Staff
October 29, 1941

Gamblers at heart

For a lot of people, the possibility of getting out of a small place and travelling in your own country or perhaps even getting overseas was very attractive. To travel, before the war, you had to have money and most people just didn't . . . and to have that desire to travel you also had to have a certain spirit of adventure, too. Most people who were attracted to the service had to be gamblers at heart, because none of us really had any conception of what it would be like. We simply took our chances.

Former officer, WRCNS

Oath of Allegiance not taken

I enlisted, as did most of the American women – we were girls, then of eighteen, nineteen, or twenty – because our armed forces did not take females under twenty-one, while the Canadian Army did. I wrote asking if Americans were accepted. I was surprised later to discover that the Canadian Army had actually recruited in Boston (among other centres) . . . The Americans did not sign the oath of allegiance. My documents read: "Oath of allegiance not taken by virtue of being a citizen of Yonkers, New York."

Former member, CWAC

Both older women . . . sons in the service

I met these two women going down to Ottawa in the same train. They were both older women who had sons in the service and evidently they'd decided that working in a munitions plant just wasn't doing enough so they'd joined the Navy themselves. And they got more than they'd bargained for, too.

I bumped into one of them some time later and it seems they'd been assigned to work as maids in the officers' mess and they were spending their time serving afternoon tea to the officers' wives. They were even too ashamed to tell their sons about it. So much for the war effort. They were prepared to do anything to get out.

Former member, WRCNS

Disgruntled women

There were a lot of disgruntled women in the services. They felt they'd got themselves into something that they couldn't get out of, unless they got themselves pregnant, or caused a lot of disruption, one way or another.

Former officer, CWAC

Certainly not to get rich

I wanted to improve myself. Before I joined the Navy, I was working for the Singer Sewing Machine Co. and I decided that rather than learn a new trade when I went in, I'd just develop the skills I already had . . . I ended up doing all the fine work on the officers' uniforms, sewing on the gold braid and so on.

Some of us left pretty darn good jobs to go into the service and even if you were "trades pay," which was always a little more – it was basically chicken feed we made. Nobody ever joined up in order to get rich, that's for sure!

Former member, WRCNS

To get away from home, period

I was in nine months and ten days exactly, and ten days after I got *in*, I decided I wanted to get *out*. My purpose in joining up was to get away from home, period! It was the routine I hated . . . I didn't like being told what to do . . . I was too independent to enjoy being in the service.

Former member, RCAF (WD)

Mother was the only slacker

My best friend was to blame . . . because she joined up in Vancouver and wrote back this glowing letter saying how wonderful things were in the Air Force. The family was pretty service-oriented, too. My brother, my father and later my younger sister were all in the service. I used to say my mother was the only slacker in the outfit.

Former member, RCAF (WD)

Runaway wife

Dear Sir or Madam:

I shall be very brief, so please bear with me for a few minutes.

Eight (8) weeks ago while employed and living in Hamilton, Ontario, I became ill with the flu and then pleurisy . . . My wife was employed as a waitress at the "Sweetheart Bar Restaurant," 164 King St. East, Hamilton, Ontario. Right after I was sent up here she was discharged from her work. I have discovered since, it was because of her character. Something or other to do with the husband whom is manager of this "Sweetheart Bar."

My wife often told me she was going to join the C.W.A.A.F.

She wrote a letter to me over four weeks ago from Toronto, "No address" saying she was leaving me because she had fallen in love with the manager of the "Sweetheart Bar."

Well, I am still confined to bed from my illness and the shock of her deserting me at a time like this when I need her help to get well again.

Not only that, but we have a little boy six years old and she left him with her aged mother with no arrangement for his support or schooling which he is starting this term. I am too ill to be able to look after anything, and her brother is lying at death's door with a poisoned leg and pneumonia, also at her mother's place where our little boy is. She is needed worse at home than anywhere else at this time.

I have tried everything to locate her, and now I am imploring you to help me if you know her whereabouts, or if she should try to enlist in the Women's Division of the R.C.A.F. or the C.W.A.A.F. at any of your Depots or perhaps already has.

This is very urgent and I beg you to help me if you can. I love my wife and I want her here at home.

Her description is: She was 24 years old on March 6, 1942. She is about 5'6" tall, medium blonde hair, wears glasses with octagon shaped lens, false upper plate in her mouth. When last seen she was wearing a New Harrison Tweed Coat; black felt sailor shaped hat with an ornamentation made of the same goods on the front of the hat "spiralled," a black tailored suit with white pin stripes, or a black dress with red trimmings, and black fur trimmed goloshes. She is very pretty of Scotch birth, but no accent whatever in her speech.

I am still confined to bed after (8) weeks of illness and this worry and grief will send me to a sanatorium if she is not found immediately.

If you can help me in any way please feel that you are doing a wonderful service to a sick man.

You have my permission to use the enclosed description of her in any way that might help me to find my wife. Please help me if you can.
P.S. If she has already enlisted then please use your own judgement in this matter.

Put together meals the way Mother used to
Woman's traditional excellence in at least one particular field – cooking –
will pay dividends in the Canadian Women's Auxiliary Air Force, now in
process of organization.

One of the first needs, when general recruiting begins, will be for cooks;
and because of this factor there is likely to be a greater opportunity for rapid
advancement in this sphere than in some of the others. All trades will offer
possibilities for promotion, but up to the present time the woman who can
put together meals the way Mother used to will have something of an edge
on her fellow volunteers.

RCAF Public Relations Release No. 459.
September 20, 1941

Enlistment is a serious business
The whispering campaign against the morality of women in the services is
largely a symptom of resentment against an innovation which is somehow
felt to be "unwomanly." Opposition will not disappear until the Women's
Services are taken completely for granted, but it can be substantially reduced
by some of the following suggestions:

1. Appeal to the spirit of sacrifice by giving full weight to the
    hardships and disadvantages of service life. "Sure, they work
    hard for small pay, and are often tired and lonely – but they are
    happy all the same, because they know they're helping their
    country."
2. Support this by a sober, frank, matter-of-fact tone in all publicity
    – enlistment is a serious business and deserves to be taken
    seriously. The coy note of most advertising addressed to women
    should be avoided; it deprives the services of all importance,
    putting them on a level with choosing a hat or angling for a date.
3. Appeal directly to the families of potential recruits: "Have any of
    your daughters joined up yet? They couldn't do anything more
    valuable."
4. Emphasize the fact that all the United Nations' women are doing
    similar service; only the Nazis, with their mediaeval views of
    women's place, exclude them from participation in the services.
5. Avoid the suggestion that service women are either in close
    contact with men – "shoulder to shoulder" – or completely cut off
    from them; emphasize the normal character of their social con-

tacts, and the fact that they have dates, get engaged and married just like anyone else.

6. Don't try to make all the service women look like Hollywood stars; that provokes dangerous reactions. Show them as they are – ordinary Canadian girls, doing an important job.

> Confidential Memorandum
> Wartime Information Board
> March 19, 1943

It was wide open

The uniformed women controversy – you know, it really was true, in spite of all the talk about the war effort and how we should all be doing our part . . . There were still lots of people who didn't approve of the idea of women being in uniform. I think some of them were men hoping their wives were at home behaving themselves. The single people . . . they could have cared less. It was wide open, really.

The worst type to deal with, from our point of view as women, were the fellows who'd been in the Army for years and were making a career

Interior of aircraft cockpit is cleaned and polished by two members of the RCAF (WD).

out of it when the war came along. They'd had so much regimentation by then, they were almost like the Gestapo. Everything was either black or white.

Former member, CWAC

So, my patriotic step-cousin

Upon arrival of your outstanding invitation to become a "Private" in the C.W.A.C.'s, I wish to inform you are a very poor recruiting officer and I assure you that if I ever decide to join up it will not be the cause of you informing of my private and personal doings . . . I don't object to you sending me information and facts about the C.W.A.C.'s but your personal letter displayed only ignorance in the best sense of the word . . . Have you ever heard a serviceman speak well of the W.D.'s, Army, Air Force, or Navy? Nine out of every ten resent having girls in uniform and my brothers said they would disown me if I ever join with such scruff.

You apparently had reasons to join up and since you had no real home, I don't blame you for being satisfied with a bunk that you can go home to when you wish. However, I am glad you feel that you are doing your part . . . For one to neglect one's Mother such as you have, is the most unGodly thing ever heard of. If your Mother means so little to you, you need not help in this Big job, for if you cannot see the best in life why would you want to help to hold it?

So my patriotic step-cousin, I am informing you that I would like you to kindly mind your own business for you will then find life and friends a little more profitable if you did so.

If you are happy in the service, very well, but it isn't everyone who can put up with that kind of life. The C.W.A.C.'s may be a good outfit, but that is yet to be seen.

Please don't lecture to me what is right and what is wrong, for you have neither the brains nor the heart to know.

Letter to a CWAC member
Edmonton, Alberta
August 8, 1944

Topless . . . in the middle of it all

A friend of mine who had volunteered for the Air Force was called up ahead of me, so she'd already been through her medical and told me what

Montreal Gazette Collection, National Archives of Canada, PA-108273

Unidentified CWAC mechanics at work in machine shop, April 3, 1942.

to expect. Well, that was fine for the Air Force, but it wasn't the Army and when I finally got called in for the medical, I thought I was all prepared. According to my friend in the Air Force, nothing was left to the imagination. Everyone had to strip and then they were gone over with a fine-toothed comb – every nook and cranny. So, I thought to myself, "I guess if they're going to make me take it all off, I might as well wear as little as possible to start with." And when they got us all assembled for our medicals they told us to take off everything except our brassieres and panties. What a sight it was too – with every different kind of get-up from bloomers to the knee to skimpy little satin and lace affairs.

And there I was in the middle of it all – topless! The medical officer came along the line and stopped at me. "Well," he said, "you came well prepared, didn't you?" I could have sunk right through the floor. As for the medical itself, I don't know what they were looking for – what medical qualifications you had to have – mostly if you could breathe, I think, because they didn't put us on a table or anything of that sort.

Former officer, CWAC

I could hear it ticking

During my medical, the doctor was testing my ears and he put his watch to my ear and asked me if I could hear it ticking, and I said no, because just at that moment, a truck was passing by the window outside and I couldn't hear a thing, naturally. I guess I should have said I could hear it because it went down on my medical records that I was deaf in one ear and that stayed on my record; right to the end of the war. I could not persuade him that it was the truck; and who knows, it might have affected my going overseas, or not?

Former member, WRCNS

I told them my birth certificate was lost

You enrolled for adventure. At seventeen, who had much experience? I lied about my age and told them my birth certificate was lost. That was in '42 when we'd already been hearing war songs for three years. I was working in Montreal and every day I had to pass a recruiting office. Take part in the war? Be a patriot? Replace a man? Perhaps . . . but for me it was really more for the fun of it and to see new places. They were great years!

Former member, CWAC
(Translation from French)

Not sailors or lumberjacks

I find it difficult to make the Army appreciate that the women selected are ladies from good homes who desire to serve their country, and are not sailors or lumberjacks picked off the street. They are not to be spoken of facetiously or to be treated with supercilious indifference. Senior officers should set an example in this respect and all must be received properly, given suitable quarters both in which to live and in which to work.

They are not successors to the "Camp followers" of the armies of the previous age. All ranks must be made to realize that they are young women of good character who are making a sacrifice to serve their Country.

The Registrar, Halifax, N.S.
for the Dept. of National War Services
October 7, 1941

Going wrong?

My decision to join the RCAF (WD) was made in February 1943 while on a trip to New Westminster, B.C., in search of employment. Having come from my home in southern Alberta where at age nineteen years, I had grown tired of four years as domestic help to neighbouring women, I had found work through Manpower, at Drakes' Dairy. My aunt, with whom I was staying, objected to the hours of my new shift and had suggested I find other accommodation as she did not want me coming in at midnight. Not knowing the city, I went back to Manpower for assistance in locating a place to stay; and during the conversation they asked if I might consider entering the forces. I subsequently returned home to Alberta and sent to Calgary for information on the CWAC, and the RCAF (WD). Having chosen the latter, I was duly sworn in on April 12, 1943, and was off to Rockcliffe Basic Training Centre the next day. My parents did not stand in my way but several of my friends had some weird stories of how "Army girls go wrong." I was even offered a proposal of marriage by my current boyfriend who was due home on leave from his Army post in Ontario. As fate would have it, I was on the train going east, and he was on the one coming west.

Former member, RCAF (WD)

To share in the excitement
As one grows older, one's perspective changes, and now, years later, it is difficult to remember how things appeared then. At the time that I joined the Wrens, I was teaching public school in a northwestern Ontario town. Another teacher, whose brother was in the Navy, became a very good friend. We were young – belonging to a Depression generation that was unworldly and naive by the standards of today's youth. The war had already been going on for some time with no end in sight. We were probably motivated by various factors – a desire to help, patriotism (the world was not so small in those days), a desire to see more of the world and share in the excitement, to get out of a rut.

Former member, WRCNS

We'll have to join
In our family there were three women (girls really) who served. Our eldest brother had joined the Royal Rifles and was among the unfortunate men who were sent to Hong Kong. When Hong Kong fell to the Japanese, my older sister said, "We'll have to join the RCAF, Mary, and do our part to help bring him home." She joined in January 1942. I had to wait until my eighteenth birthday in July 1942. Later, another sister, Edna, joined the

Army. This was after we had received word of the death of our brother.

The war tore our family apart and we still carry scars deep in our hearts.

Former member, RCAF (WD)

Funeral march for CWAC Cpl. Olive Walker, Ottawa, Ont., May 14, 1943.

Canadian Forces Photographic Unit, DND, PL-11316

RCAF (WD) recruits from Calgary boarding train for Manning Depot in Ontario.

Molly Lamb Bobak, *Winnipeg Train Station*, February 1, 1943.

THREE

Preparing to Serve

H AVING ONCE SIGNED ON ITS recruits, each of the women's services was faced with the task of preparing them for life in uniform as members of Canada's armed forces. The task of outfitting, training, and generally "processing" its newcomers to the military fold was, of necessity, to be accomplished with efficiency, as quickly and effectively as was humanly possible. Uniforms and accommodation would have to be provided. The intricacies of the fine art of marching and drill would have to be introduced. And into each and every glowing heart, a sense of the traditions of the service must be firmly implanted. The importance of being part of a military community, of doing one's duty, of discipline and pride must be stressed if the militarization of Canada's women was to be a success.

Here again each service performed these minor miracles according to its own traditions and organizational structure. The CWAC, with the largest number of servicewomen in its ranks, set up two centres for the purpose of training between 350 and 430 women each month; one in Vermilion, Alberta, and the other in Kitchener, Ontario. The Air Force established training facilities with similar capacity in both Toronto and Ottawa, while virtually every probationary member of the WRCNS went through the rigours of induction into the Senior Service under the watchful eye of Lt. Commander Isabel J. Macneill, O.B.E., at HMCS *Conestoga* (known as the Stone Frigate) in Galt (Cambridge), Ontario.

National Archives of Canada, PA-146020

Personnel of WRCNS undergoing drill on the parade ground during Basic Training at HMCS Conestoga, Galt, Ont., December 1942.

The original organization of the CWAC was undertaken by Matron-in-Chief Col. Elizabeth Smellie, C.B.E., a highly qualified and capable woman who had served overseas as a Canadian nursing sister during the First World War. As temporary officer administrating, she was detailed to select the women who would act as the corps' officers. A trans-Canada tour included calls on the commandants of local women's volunteer organizations and this in turn provided the Canadian Women's Army Corps with a nucleus of well-qualified leaders. By their own admission, many of these women, despite their experience as members of paramilitary groups, were not quite prepared for the transition to the "real" army, but they learned quickly and well.

After providing an invaluable service to the corps at its inception, Matron Smellie stepped down in November 1941, and direction of the corps fell to Joan Barbara Kennedy, formerly a pillar of the 1938 volunteer corps in Victoria, B.C. A subsequent reorganization of the chain of command in 1943 created a division of responsibilities; Joan Kennedy was placed in charge of training, while Lt. Colonel Margaret Eaton, as assistant adjutant-general, co-ordinated all other CWAC matters. In effect, this left the CWAC without an official head until April 1944, when Margaret Eaton was promoted to acting colonel and director-general of the CWAC. When appointed she was only thirty-one, but had more than proved her worth many times over.

Both the Navy and the Air Force relied on senior British WRNS and WAAF personnel advisors for guidance in the organization and instruction of their fledgling trainees. In the original hierarchy of the Canadian Women's Auxiliary Air Force, two Canadians were appointed, Kathleen Walker, formerly head of the Ottawa Branch of the Red Cross Motor Transport Corps, and Dr. Jean Davey. Their duties included the selection and training of the Air Force's "first 150." Following completion of a five-week intensive and demanding introduction to the RCAF, the participants were either granted commissions or given the rank of NCO in the CWAAF, and were sent forth from the former premises of Havergal College, a private Toronto girls' school on Jarvis Street, to assume their assigned roles.

The Navy's first Canadian headquarters appointment to the WRCNS was Captain Adelaide Helen Grant Sinclair, O.B.E., who had previously been an official for the Wartime Prices and Trade Board. Captain Sinclair served as director of the Women's Royal Canadian Naval Service after having trained in England with the British WRNS. When Captain Dorothy Isherwood returned to England in September 1943, Adelaide Sinclair took command and served admirably in that capacity for the duration of the war.

The first class of WRCNS recruits graduated from Kingsmill House in Ottawa after receiving Basic Training for one month, commencing August 29, 1942. There were sixty-seven in this original group of Canadian Wrens and twenty-two of them were commissioned as officers of His Majesty's Royal Canadian Navy – the first women to carry the King's commission in any of the British Commonwealth's naval services.[1]

The duration of Basic Training was between four and six weeks for a woman in the service, compared to an average of eight weeks for a uniformed male. Initially, even officer training in the CWAC was limited to a one-month stint at Ste. Anne-de-Bellevue, but after much agitation on the part of Colonel Joan Kennedy this was extended to eight weeks and involved more intensive preparation for duty as an officer.

It was to be borne in mind at all times, however, that "the primary function of the CWAC is to release soldiers for more active duty."[2]

The matter of who would be the most effective instructors in the actual process of training female personnel gave rise to any number of contrary opinions. The case for leaving the instruction of female recruits in the infinitely more experienced (ergo more capable) hands of uniformed males was eloquently presented in a brief to the decision-makers:

> It is felt that women will take more kindly to instruction in military subjects from an experienced male officer or soldier than they will from one of their own sex ... as they are quick to realize that the latter personnel can have only a very limited background.[3]

Moreover, the selection of "good officer material" was vital to the success of any training program in the forces. The women who became officers and NCOs – often with only a minimum of preparation for the responsibilities they would have to shoulder – were expected to take the job seriously. They were to perform their duties using their disciplinary powers to the full, but to temper these powers with a healthy dose of common sense. If they could command respect and instil pride in those who served in the ranks, they were only doing what was expected of them.

During officer training, they became familiar with military protocol and nomenclature. For example, an officer candidate would have to know whether or not the rider of a cycle (pedal or motor) or the driver of a mechanical vehicle should salute while the vehicle was in motion. (Answer: negative – due to the danger of taking his/her eyes off the road.)

She would also have to answer such questions as: If three servicewomen are walking down the street together and they meet an officer, do they all salute? (Answer: the one on the right only.) Or, do you remove your hat when entering (1) a church, (2) an office, (3) a theatre? (Answer: an office.)

These officers and NCOs of the future also required instruction in dealing with practicalities such as which foot to give the halt command on when marching in quick time and how to fill out the multitudinous records for postings, promotions, release from the service and so forth that made up what was known as the "paper war."

Members of RCAF (WD) take a cigarette break.

It was impressed upon all potential officers that every grievance, however small, must be set right or remedied. It was the best way to ensure good morale, and to this end a chain of complaint was set up in order that grievances could never be suppressed.

Officer trainees in the RCAF (WD), for instance, were warned that "a discontented airwoman is contagious, and you don't want epidemics of that kind."[4]

Every officer had to possess a thorough knowledge and understanding of the rules and regulations she would have to enforce (in every conceivable circumstance) – rules about protocol, about smoking, about the consumption of intoxicants in public and elsewhere. She would have to rely from time to time on the force's disciplinary unit: the Service Police, Provost Corps, or Shore Patrol – whose role was defined as "taking the pot off the stove before it boils over."

And this cautionary maxim was to be absorbed and heeded: "Discipline based on brute force and fear is evil and is the discipline of the slave . . . but without discipline, an organization, a service, or a nation becomes a disorganized rabble."[5]

Canadian Forces Photographic Unit, DND, PL-24004

Officers were expected to set an example in every aspect of their bearing and behaviour. They were to be, in effect, an inspiration and had to take a personal interest in each and every one of those women serving under their command: "Some will need encouragement, others restraint. Some will find service life difficult, others will make mistakes. Try to understand them all and help them. This will take time, thought and sympathy."[6]

Orders were to be carefully considered before being given, and only issued if they were "necessary, lawful, reasonable and fair."

Favouritism was to be avoided at all costs and reprimands were to be tactful – firm, but human.

NCOs were to serve as a link between officers and the rank and file and should never become a barrier to the development of "team spirit." The force was, after all, a vast machine and "certain cogs in that machine are now women – instead of men."[7]

When it came to inspection of troops, definite standards were to be adhered to. An officer's or NCO's eagle eye should be capable, in a heartbeat, of detecting unpolished shoes, twisted stockings, or hair below the collar, to say nothing of skirts that were not regulation length, tunics with tarnished buttons or pockets that bulged unnaturally, makeup that was "conspicuous," hats and ties that were askew, and so on and on.

Instruction in drill procedure was yet another aspect of officer training right down to the correct measured length for each specific marching pace. In the WDs a side pace, for example, was to be precisely twelve inches; stepping forward or back, twenty-seven inches; slow march, thirty inches; whereas the pace for "stepping out" increased to thirty-three inches and "double march" to forty.

Not only were the paces measured, but they had to be executed in specific numbers of paces per minute, starting at seventy paces per minute for slow time and accelerating to 180 for double time (around 200 yards per minute). Hardly a snail's pace!

Each officer candidate was imbued, as well, with healthy respect for the old adage that the pen is mightier than the sword. Directives from headquarters made it clear that "communication with the press is forbidden without special authority."[8]

Every officer was granted a fixed amount ($150) for the purchase of her uniform and was advised that her skirt length had to measure exactly sixteen inches from the ground. High heels, petticoats, and scarves were strictly taboo. Gloves were to be either worn or carried in the left hand at all times and at no time would an officer carry a bag, an umbrella, or a cane, let alone be seen wearing any sort of fur. Jewellery was limited to engagement and wedding ring (small stones only) and signet-type rings.[9]

Whatever major or minor luxuries an officer might have grown accustomed to in her life as a civilian had to be put aside for the duration of her stint in uniform. The same, of course, applied to those who served in the ranks. Dedication to duty was the order of the day – minus any discernible frills.

"Special problems" were to be dealt with by the officer in charge with humanity, but also with dispatch. And woe betide any servicewoman who contracted VD. The standing order was that she must report this distressing fact without delay. Concealment of VD was to be dealt with under the appropriate military act. Deserters and those who were listed as absent without leave were to have their clothing, necessaries, and accoutrements placed in safe custody. Following this, an inventory (in triplicate) was to be compiled and once the offender was declared a deserter, her kit could be reissued, after cleaning and repairs (with the cost of same charged to the guilty party).

The making of a good officer was clearly essential to the success and effectiveness of the force, but it was a demanding and onerous responsibility. Small wonder that a good many women elected to take orders in preference to dispensing them and following them through. Officer status may have carried with it a degree of prestige, respect, and deference, but those who bore it were also presented with more than their share of headaches in the execution of their role as officer in His Majesty's Armed Forces.

Women serving in the ranks, the women who were issued orders and were expected to carry them out to the letter, required specialized training and preparation for their new role. Switching to life in the military was not simply a matter of climbing out of one's seamed nylons and high-heeled pumps and into a uniform. It involved a carefully devised program of integration – some would prefer the term indoctrination – and in the eyes of some of those selected, it marked the beginning of depersonalization on a grand scale. Certainly the patriotic fervour of the recruits arriving for their "Basic" was put to the test in very short order. Perhaps even the young woman who reported for Basic Training with WE HAVE TO KILL THE GERMANS AND THE JAPS emblazoned on her valise may occasionally have had second thoughts about the wisdom of her choice. It was no life for those devoid of a sense of humour; nor, for that matter, was it a life for anyone who could not adapt to almost any circumstance or situation.

It was intended that during Basic Training the wheat would be well sifted from the chaff in order that only those women who could "take it" would remain in the service. Even at that, a few "undesirables" did manage to slip through the net. This, however, appears to have been much more the exception than the rule. Despite rumours of a "prostitute invasion," the morals and character of the vast majority of women who volunteered for service in the uniform of their country were indisputably of the highest order.

The first of the practicalities involved in Basic Training was the transport of recruits to the centres set up for their instruction. Nor were the arrangements for this always as uncomplicated as they might have been. The need to provide escorts for groups of young women travelling long distances to their designated destinations by rail was soon brought to the attention of those in command.

Canadian Forces Photographic Unit, DND, PL-14757

Recruits for the RCAF (WD) wait beside their bus (location unknown).

The first RCAF (WD) group to arrive for duty at Claresholm, Alta., 1942.

MEMORANDUM

Escorts for W.D. Recruits

1. During my recent inspection trip of Western Canada a subject of some concern brought forward was the deportment of newly enlisted young women, travelling to the Manning Depots. It was the consensus of opinion that an escort was required to maintain discipline. The unaccustomed

freedom of these enlisted girls, some of them leaving home for the first time, very often finds expression in behaviour which is unbecoming to the personnel of the Air Force. This youthful spirit is understandable especially when they come in contact with other inexperienced airwomen bound for the same destination.[10]

Having arrived safe and sound to commence Basic Training, what might have remained of a recruit's civilian status was swiftly supplanted by her new identity as a member of the service and by a bunk which would be her home away from home until she was assigned to a more permanent placement upon completion of her "Basic."

In due course she was also issued her uniform and kit:

Uniforms for Officers and other ranks will be similar in design and detail. As in the Army, Officers on appointment or promotion will receive an allowance for uniform and equipment.

Volunteers on enrolment will be issued with clothing, badges and equipment as follows: headdress; skirts and tunics; shirts with attached collars; tie; stockings; greatcoat and waterproof; brown leather shoes and gloves; rubbers; lightweight pullover sweater; overalls; also cap and shoulder badges, haversack and water bottle.

Articles such as aprons, working denim overalls, mitts, gauntlets and other equipment required for special employment will be issued as required.

Underclothing, toilet articles and necessaries will not be issued but an allowance of $15.00 for this purpose will be granted on enrolment, with an additional $3.00 quarterly.[11]

From the start, the selection and design of a suitable uniform was a continuing bone of contention in all three services. In a letter from Westmount, Quebec, to Mme. Thérèse Casgrain (the political activist who led the campaign for women's rights in Quebec), an anonymous civilian expressed her very definite views on the subject of a uniform for the Canadian Women's Army Corps with appropriate vehemence:

Dear Madam,

Please excuse me, a stranger to you, for taking the liberty of writing to you, but knowing from your splendid radio talks your active sympathy in all that concerns women, I wish to enlist your interest in the matter of uniforms to be issued to the Women's Army Corps, which I hope to join.

I do hope that *before it is too late to do anything about it* someone of importance, such as yourself, will insist that this uniform be modern, smart, and becoming in both design and colour.

The newspapers talk of Khaki – a colour most unbecoming to almost every woman. Why not gray? It is becoming to most people. (That at present worn by the Voluntary Women's Service Corps of the Red Cross is very nice.)

Again they say the proposed uniform has been designed by a military officer at Headquarters, Ottawa, and add that he is a married man. This uniform should be designed by a proper *couturier,* subject to military approval. They talk of a suit – coat and skirt – designed on the lines of an officer's tunic (stout women look awful in them), plus a shirt-waist with collar and tie like a man's.

Don't you agree with me that since a women's corps is an innovation it is silly to slavishly follow the old idea of the men's army uniform with their throttling collars and ties – the men themselves discard these articles the moment they get the chance. Then why wish them on women who are accustomed to having their throats free?

My suggestion is that instead of a suit, the uniform should be a *dress,* cut on the current popular "shirtwaist dress" lines with long sleeves; they are becoming to everybody, practical, comfortable and smart. If desired, a detachable soft white linen collar could be added for smartness and clean appearance; and a military belt could give the necessary military touch with rank insignia on shoulder, breast pocket, or sleeve.

. . .(Ease of adjustment as to size is important, nothing looks worse than a woman in a suit too large or too small for her, and once issued, it may not be easy to get a suit adjusted.)

As to headgear, those "chauffeur" caps look just hideous on all but the most attractive girls. Why not a neat, tailored felt such as the nursing sisters wear; most women look well in them?

Please excuse the length of this letter, but no woman likes to look ugly or ridiculous.[12]

And in Ottawa where various possibilities for the CWAC uniform were under consideration, there was almost equal consternation. An officer involved in the decision-making process claims that the original costume modelled for the minister of national defence, Colonel Ralston, and his wife, was found distinctly wanting on several counts. The consensus was that while it might be becoming for a hotel hat-check girl, it was definitely unsuitable for its intended purpose.

National Archives of Canada, PA-129068

Col. J.L. Ralston returning from England, is greeted at Rockcliffe Airport by two CWAC recruits: Misses Jones and Brown, Ottawa, Ont.

Following the rejection of this initial attempt, a Toronto designer, Jack Creed, was commissioned by Col. Victor Sifton, the master general of ordnance, to create a new model – stipulating only that the greatcoat be cut on the lines of pre-war cavalry officers' coats. Mr. Creed did his best, but even his efforts did not please everyone and a DND HQ committee was set up to modify Mr. Creed's design. When presented with the changes, the designer was distraught almost to the point of tears, but the committee's decisions provided the CWAC with the uniform its members would wear for the duration of the war.[13]

Almost within hours of arrival at Basic Training, every new recruit was subjected to another cursory physical inspection and a series of unwelcome but necessary inoculations. On occasion, there would be an outbreak of head lice – that dread condition of the scalp so fondly described by generations of children as "cooties." When this occurred, each newcomer's scalp was thoroughly examined and the results duly tabulated. The "cootie code" devised by the CWAC for this purpose was divided into five gradations: one X represented the presence of up to ten nits; two X's denoted up to fifty; three and four X's stood for fairly numerous and very numerous; five indicated (horrors!) live lice. A supplementary code used symbols to record the duration and seriousness of the infestation. The letter A represented live nits as observed through a magnifying glass and the letter D, appropriately, indicated that whatever was there was at least dead.[14]

When deemed necessary, de-infestation measures were taken immediately if not sooner. Mattresses and pillows were disinfected, and the unfortunates who were found to be contaminated (many of the women who had worked in war plants had been required to wear head scarves, which served as excellent incubators for nits) were rendered conspicuous by virtue of the oily treatment which was applied promptly to their heads and left there for several days.

Aside from marching and drill and the joys of inoculation, the most memorable aspect of Basic Training appears to have been the daily routine of scrubbing and polishing floors, windows, latrines, and every other surface in or out of sight that was remotely scrubbable. Then, there were the pot-bellied stoves that embellished, though they barely heated, many of the buildings that were used to house the trainees. These had to be fed, stoked, and cleaned out regularly and this, too, became part of the daily round and common task.

In terms of psychological impact, the realities encountered during this introduction to military life certainly left their mark. Two of the most common shocks for most women were the complete lack of privacy and the total regimentation of their lives from the minute they clambered out of their bunks each morning. In all probability, there were many young male soldiers whose experiences were similar, but it is possible that they were somewhat more prepared for the onslaught, by virtue of centuries of military tradition and its association with men and bloodshed. Men must be prepared to "take it like a man"; whereas women, having no prior conditioning, were, as one former servicewoman put it, "just like babes in the woods ... feeling our way as we went along." Unless she had experienced communal living at a boarding school or summer camp or was a member of an inordinately large family, the average recruit was less than prepared for her new way of life. The shock of having to abandon almost every vestige of one's personal identity for a regulated and impersonal existence in the militia was something that was totally unforeseen by most women who enlisted – until it was too late.

Those women who managed to endure the rigours of Basic Training then proceeded to the next phase in their service career. The women selected for officer training were subsequently assigned various postings across the country or overseas, while many of those in the ranks were dispersed to receive more specialized training in a trade or occupation over a longer period, often up to six months. Originally the number of these trades and occupations was very low. There were, in fact, only eight or nine possible categories at the outset and the majority of these were related to office or clerical functions.

Women who were willing to train as cooks or fabric workers were in great demand and the category of MT (mechanized transport) became the choice of many trainees. The categories of general duties and messwoman seem to have been a sort of catch-all for anyone who could not be slotted into any other type of work. In late 1941, the CWAAF outlined its qualification requirements for these original categories very clearly.

Clerks

(a) *Accounting*

Candidates must have at least two year's High School education. They must hold a certificate of education from a High School of Commerce or other recognized business college, or alternatively have two years' business experience with a firm of repute. In accounting, including the handling of books of accounting and of stock records, a knowledge of typing, filing and office routine is to be preferred. Personnel whose only credential is graduation from a business college must additionally have at least one year's office experience to be given preference.

(b) *General*

Candidates must have a knowledge of typing, filing and office routine. Graduation from a recognized business college can be considered satisfactory, but candidates with a minimum of three years' office experience will be given preference.

(c) *Stenographers*

Candidates must be able to take dictation at 100 words per minute, and type 40 words per minute. They must be good, clear penwomen and be able to transcribe clear, concise English from rough notes. They must be familiar with filing systems and general office procedure.

Cooks
Candidates must have a knowledge of and interest in cooking. Candidates will be given a course of six weeks at a special cooking school.

Dental Assistant
Candidates must have experience assisting at the chair in a Dental Office.

Driver (Transport)
Candidates must show a recognized motor mechanic's certificate, such as General Motors, Ford, Technical Schools, etc. They must be in possession of a provincial automobile driver's permit, currently active. They must have a clear understanding of the provincial highway traffic act, covering driving speeds, passing, parking and accident procedure for the home district. Preference will be given to drivers who have the widest driving experience.

Equipment Assistant
Candidates should have had experience of stockroom handling, and have a knowledge of storing methods for inflammable and easily damaged goods. They should be good, accurate penwomen with some bookkeeping or clerical experience and some ability in packing and crating.

Fabric Worker
Candidates should be strong, intelligent women with experience in sewing. Those with experience in operating power-driven sewing machines will be given preference. Training as tailors or upholsterers is desirable but not essential. Candidates must be strong and healthy and keen to tackle a job which is interesting but which often entails rough work.

Hospital Assistant
Candidates must have some training as a "Trained Attendant" or hold a St. John Ambulance or Red Cross certificate. They will be called up to do the same duties as nurses in training. Preference will be given to candidates who have had training in recognized services.

Operator, Telephone
Candidates must have a good speaking voice and enunciation, have experience in operating a switchboard. They must be courteous, reliable and discreet. Preference will be given to those with wide experience.

Standard

(a) *General Duties*

Candidates must be of a type suitable for general employment and domestic duties. They must be strong and accustomed to hard work. They will be employed on cleaning duties in offices, work-rooms, dining halls and club houses, and as messengers and runners.

(b) *Messwomen*

Candidates must be of a type suitable for general employment as messwomen. Preference will be given to experienced waitresses and domestic servants.

CWAC personnel servicing a tank at Longue Pointe, Que., Ordnance Depot, April 20, 1944.

RCAF (WD) Sergeant K.W. Horsman of Toronto leaving aircraft after familiarization flight. (No.3.S.F.T.S. Calgary, Alberta.)

APPLICANTS ARE STRONGLY URGED NOT TO RELINQUISH THEIR CIVILIAN EMPLOYMENT UNTIL THEY HAVE BEEN DEFINITELY AC-CEPTED BY THE RCAF AND HAVE NOTIFICATION IN WRITING OF THE DATE THEY ARE TO PROCEED TO THE TRAINING DEPOT.

CWAAF directive

By the war's end the list of trade training possibilities for servicewomen had expanded almost beyond belief from the original eight or nine categories to well over fifty trades and occupations. As well, the rates of pay had been readjusted to equal that of a man performing a similar function.

Women began to acquire unforeseen skills, many of them skills that had previously been part and parcel of the male territorial imperative: telegraphers, radio operators, draughtsmen, mechanics, and technicians with specialized expertise in precision instruments, radio operations and so on. As more and more men were required for combat and overseas duty, more and more women were needed to help fill in the gaps.

Canadian Forces Photographic Unit, DND, PL-16135

*Airwomen Gillis of Bathurst, N.B., B. Jennex (left) of Halifax,
and V. Hipkiss of Toronto take time out for a mock wedding party.*

Early in January 1943, the possibility of training women as pilots was presented to the war committee of the Cabinet; however, the proposal was not ratified. On the other hand, the committee was prepared to re-open discussion with the Air Council in six months' time. Nothing further came of the idea, but the original proposal is, in itself, an indication of the inroads made by members of the RCAF Women's Division in terms of proficiency and competence.[15]

In a good many instances, though, the tasks assigned to women were humdrum and routine to the point of distraction. To their credit, for the most part the women who performed these jobs accepted the monotony with good-natured resignation. If it was tiresome and dreary work it still meant that another man was being freed for active duty.

This point was pressed home whenever possible, partly to hearten the weary and dispirited, but also to promote the cause of an improved public image for women in uniform. The contribution of these women to the war effort must somehow receive the recognition it deserved. An RCAF officer quoted in the press was obviously attempting to get his message across when he wrote:

Take the routine folding of a parachute. For a man it is tiresome routine work – especially when he's just waiting for a chance to get into the air with a parachute strapped to his back. But for a woman it's different. She is in a position to save a life – maybe her husband's or fiancé's – who knows? And so she takes a very special interest in her work and probably does it with much greater diligence and devotion than a frustrated flier would.

La Presse, August 1, 1943
(author's translation)

Then again, the women who had been trained to fold the parachutes were never interviewed, so any true assessment of their on-the-job motivation is impossible. The fact remains that, whatever the job, these women did it well. In many cases they outperformed their male counterparts and completely confounded the statisticians who had pronounced that it would take at least three women to accomplish the same amount of work as two men in an equal amount of time. Once she had received the appropriate training, a servicewoman did the job as well as, if not better than, a man, and in the face of considerably greater odds.

Notebook

Mixed with some surprises
Most trade instruction has been given in either all-male or all-female classes. Some, however, were mixed – with some surprises. In the first mixed equipment class (60 male, 40 female), Airwoman Second Class H. McLeod won the gold medal. The first time a WD was sent to the officers' administration course, Flight Officer M.O. Meredith finished at the top of her class. There are other similar cases.

RCAF Report
June 2, 1944

A rather rough go
We arrived in our "civvies," with suitcase in hand, and the next day we were outfitted . . . trotted round to get our blankets issued and our uniforms and bits and pieces. Then we lined up in a queue for our shots, four of them, two in each arm, about the second day we were there. And

of course lots of people had reactions. The barracks that night was really quite a mess because it made some people feel really sick and others got very hyper so all in all it was a rather rough go . . .

Then they marched us down to Rockcliffe to have our photographs taken for our identity cards and it had snowed that day and we all got rather wet. After that they marched us back to the drill hall and the corporal who marched us back went and changed her clothes and her wet shoes and let us stand there. Then she went to tell the officer that we were there and it always seemed to me that was very bad form on her part. Surely she should have taken the authority upon herself to send us back to change instead of letting us just stand there . . . Of course a lot of people got colds and had frozen ears. I can remember people going around with home-made cottonwool earmuffs that winter.

Former RCAF (WD)

Weeding out

You had to be a good sport. If you weren't, then you'd never make it. And part of the Basic Training we got – all that scrubbing and cleaning and polishing and drilling – was to weed out the people who couldn't take it.

Former member, WRCNS

Survival techniques

All it was, really, was to see whether or not you had the guts for life in the service. The idea was to make you so physically tired that you didn't know whether you were coming or going half the time. You learned fast how to look after yourself. God help you if you didn't. The survival techniques were the first thing you learned, right from the first meal where you had to grab your knife and take some butter as you were slinging your leg over the bench to sit down or the butter would be gone.

Former member, CWAC

To see how much you could take

A lot of people really didn't want to become officers at all; even if they had the opportunity or the ability. It just didn't have great appeal, somehow . . . And it was rigorous, that officer training course at Ste. Anne's. About two months of it. I was there in January and February '43. You had a lot of duties. You might be orderly officer during the night, but that didn't matter. You were expected to carry on just the same during the day and sometimes even on the double. They really tested your mettle to see how much you could take. To make sure you could work under pressure. And they made certain you weren't with any buddies. The idea was to mix you up so that everyone was on their own. There were four of us to a room and some were real Army types, too. Took it all very seriously – maybe a little too seriously for my taste.

Former officer, CWAC

The tears streamed down her face

Our six weeks in Basic Training were lonely weeks but we were kept busy with drills, rules, being outfitted in uniform, and mess hall duty. However, to this day there remain in my memory two things which take me back forty years – the mournful sound of the train whistle and the singing of "Ave Maria." During our training, our squad staged a talent show one afternoon and anyone with talent was asked to take part. I particularly recall one girl, her name was Geraldine, and as she sang "Ave Maria" (it was beautiful) the tears streamed down her face; the train whistled in the distance and I doubt there was a dry eye in the place as the feeling of homesickness welled up in each one of us. Next day, Geraldine went

WRCNS personnel at Gloucester, Ont., Naval Station, March 1945.

Courtesy Frances Gage, private collection

AWOL. I never saw her again and often wondered about her. Did she receive a discharge? Was she brought back and disciplined? Did she come back on her own and go through a later "boot camp"?

Former member, RCAF (WD)

All the calls were collect

The first five days we were at Rockcliffe, we weren't allowed out, but finally, Saturday night, a group of us went off to the Chateau (Laurier) and after dinner made a bee-line for the public telephones to call home. All the calls were collect, of course. "Oh yes, everything's wonderful ... I'm having a good time. We all feel well ... I'll call you next week, goodbye!" Then, the minute we hung up, everyone burst into tears, but we certainly weren't going to let on to our families that we were *homesick*.

Former member, RCAF (WD)

You didn't have any mother, either

I wasn't really toughened up enough for Basic Training ... but you just couldn't be sick. If you had a cold or a headache ... it didn't matter ... you had to get on with it ... and you didn't have any mother either. A lot of people were homesick ... and *mail* meant so much.

Former member, WRCNS

Bathing suit in the shower

In Basic Training, if you hadn't been able to laugh, you wouldn't have been able to retain your sanity. In fact, there were a few that didn't. There was one woman, a very academic, sensitive type, with her Ph.D. in something or other. I heard that she'd wear her bathing suit into the shower.

Former member, WRCNS

Ridiculous sights

When people finally started getting their uniforms, most of us looked rather funny. We really did! And we walked funny too! The shoes were all made for flat-footed people, I think ... The hats were all cut out of the same round of navy-blue felt and if you had a big head, you had a small brim; and if you had a small head, you had a huge brim; which made for some ridiculous sights.

Former officer, WRCNS

Smart and appropriate dress

Recruits naturally have a feeling of self-consciousness when first getting into Service dress, which is always accentuated by an ill-fitting uniform, so that every care is to be taken to provide well-fitting garments. In order to ensure that all items of dress are smart and appropriate, a leading stylist is being commissioned to make any modifications of dress which may be considered desirable, the objective being to provide a Service dress which personnel will in all respects be proud to wear. Any items which do not measure up to the required standards will be altered or replaced by a more appropriate article.

Confidential Report #C451710 (p.3)

August 29, 1942

Princess Alice and CWAC officer.

Decent white shirts with double cuffs

We got our uniforms in Basic Training the same day we got all our first round of shots for everything under the sun. Then you'd spend more than half your first month's pay getting your uniform to fit you properly, like buying decent white shirts with double cuffs and that sort of thing.

Former member, WRCNS

Princess Alice's help

One of my friends told me that while she was stationed in Ottawa, she and several other WDs were ordered to report to the governor general's residence. They were on Basic Training at Rockcliffe at the time . . . it was supposed to be an afternoon tea. They were picturing themselves hanging around, eating dainty little cream cheese and cucumber sandwiches; and, lo and behold, when they got there, they were told they couldn't mingle with the guests and were sent out to the scullery and given a big scrub brush and some kind of soap that would take the skin right off your hands.

There they were all scrubbing away when this friend of mine said to herself, "What would Daddy say, if he could see me now?" So she rose up off her haunches and went to protest, saying that she hadn't enlisted in His Majesty's Forces of the Royal Canadian Air Force Women's Division to scrub floors in the governor general's residence. There was a great stir caused by all this and she was put "on charge" for insubordination or something. As it turned out, "Daddy" was a very, very highly placed civil servant and threatened to go to the newspapers if this sort of thing was ever repeated. No daughter of his was going to provide cheap labour for Princess Alice's household!

Former member, RCAF (WD)

I wasn't exactly a spring chicken

All the new groups came into HMCS *Conestoga* in Galt, Ontario, on a Thursday, by train. We were picked up at the station in something that looked like an old hearse. When I arrived there, I wasn't exactly a spring chicken. I was thirty and my major concern was that I'd probably be the oldest probationary Wren in the place. I was surprised (pleasantly) to discover that there were plenty of others in my age group. There were people in their twenties, thirties, and forties . . . even a few in their fifties if they were in the cook category, where they made a few exceptions about age limits.

My first night at Galt, I had an upper bunk, and there I was with my arm full of shots. It was so sore, I had to sit up in bed to roll over and I said to myself, "My Lord, what have I gotten myself into? I'm a wreck!" Fortunately, Isabel MacNeill, the captain of our ship, was a super sales-woman. She sold us on the Navy and I don't think there was a girl who left Galt without being infused with pride at having chosen the Navy. Some-how, she managed to inspire us – callow souls, most of us – and we never let go of that feeling.

Former officer, WRCNS

Am I going to get thin in the Air Force!

The arrival was a shock enough. When you saw the bunks you were going to have to sleep in – two and a half feet wide and then when you lay down, you sank down to the floor on those glorious springs. The next morning the corporal marched us all over to the mess hall. Nobody ever explained about the *mess hall* which was a mess! You got in line and you went up and they gave you one of those thick white plates and on it they put a hard-boiled white egg . . . all very unappetizing. My first thought was, "My, am I going to get thin in the Air Force!" Then you went over and sat down at a table where there were large stacks of bread. You soon learned to take the second piece down because the top piece was stale. Then there was what we called red jam or yellow jam. I think it came from the sweepings of the E.D. Smith Co. It came in big wooden buckets. It was almost nothing but sugar and colouring.

Former member, RCAF (WD)

I got head lice too!

Because people came from so many different types of homes and families, there was a real range of standards when it came to things like cleanliness – taking baths, for example. There were some pretty bad cases of B.O. when we first arrived at Basic Training. And, to my horror, I got head lice too. Many of us did! I wanted to run away. It really did upset me. You could always tell who had them because you had to put this stuff on your head and it gave your hair a special kind of oily look . . . Oh, it was awful!

Former member, WRCNS

"Don't Fence Me In"

I remember the first song I ever heard walking into that canteen was

"Don't Fence Me In." I'll never forget that because I did feel a little fenced in, I'll tell you. So many people sitting down at once and eating, was really strange to me.

Former member, CWAC

Cold macaroni

They processed people like a sausage machine. You got your medical, did your aptitude test and were classified and slotted. Then you were sworn in and told to report on such-and-such a date. Four or six of us from Hamilton got on the slow train to Ottawa. It took most of the day to get there and when we got in, I'll never forget it, what did they serve us for dinner but cold macaroni with gravy on top of it! There were no cooks on duty and nobody seemed to have realized that after travelling all day we might need a hot meal, especially after no lunch to speak of on the train. That was probably one of my first disappointments after having joined up. It all seemed lacking in organization, somehow. Of course there were many more to come, that was just the beginning. I lay in my bunk that night thinking, "What have I done?" . . . I really did! All these years later it still makes me cross to think of our reception at Rockcliffe that night.

Former member, RCAF (WD)

Bars on our windows

One of the things that sticks in my mind from the first impressions I had of Basic Training in Galt was the bars on our windows. It had been a place for wayward girls before the Navy took it over . . . But it was a great place to train because they had lots of land.

Former member, WRCNS

We darn near starved

When I joined up, they didn't have the uniforms ready . . . so we just wore a red armband. We had our indoctrination up at a building near the Royal Ontario Museum, and during our Basic we had to live on our subsistence allowance, because they didn't have any place to put us. We were allowed $8 a week, besides our 90 cents a day. We darn near starved! The house I lived in was on St. George Street just above Bloor, one of those big old homes that the people ran as sort of a private hotel. It even had a butler, George. Six of us lived there in the attic.

Former member, CWAC

All officer candidates should complete Basic Training
Policy has now been established requiring all officer candidates to have completed satisfactory Basic Training either at existing training centres or under duly authorized district arrangements prior to the opening of the Basic Training Centres. However, there are a number of officers who "qualified" in the early courses at Ste. Anne's without taking any Basic Training. Many of these were directly commissioned from civilian life. It is felt that all officer candidates should complete basic training and serve a definite period as another rank before being selected for an officer course. Only in this way can they hope to understand the other rank's view-point.

Memo from D.N.D. (H.Q.)
Regarding CWAC Training – June 8, 1943

Off to the ladies' finishing school
The officer I worked for decided that I was officer material, so he put me up for a commission. Then I had to go through the various boards. For instance, they'd bring you in and sit you in a chair and there'd be six or eight officers (mostly men) behind a great table. Then questions would be fired at you, followed by a written test. After that we took an officer training course (along with the men) and finally we were sent off to the "Ladies' Finishing School" in Ottawa. They'd bring in a guest almost every day and give us a certain degree of "polish," so that you could conduct yourself correctly in a ward room setting with male officers and learn how to squire around important guests and be gracious and so on. Part of our training as officers also involved a lecture on how to advise our Wrens about avoiding pregnancy . . . to tell them to keep away from bushes and not to go into a hotel room with a man, and on and on . . .

Former officer, WRCNS

In a becoming and lady-like manner
As the general public judges the Service by the individuals with whom they come in contact, Women's Division recruits are to be impressed immediately on enlistment, with the responsibility devolving on them as members of the Service, as to their deportment, dress and general behaviour. Periodic talks are to be given at basic training centres, and at different stages of the Service career, urging personnel to remember that they are at all times in the public eye. Matters which may seem trivial, such as holding hands with airmen when walking out, and habitually frequenting public beverage

rooms, attract unfavourable comment, and are to be avoided. Personnel are to be impressed at all times to behave in a becoming and lady-like manner.

Confidential Report, RCAF (WD) #C451710 (p.3)

August 29, 1942

Crawling into other people's beds

We were halfway through training one group when a bunch of them came to me in a delegation to complain about one of the girls who kept crawling into other people's beds with them and couldn't something be done about it because they were sick of it. Well, I reported her, and the next thing I knew, she'd been drafted to England. They just didn't seem to want to deal with the problem. It was easier to send her away and let someone else worry about it.

Former instructor, WRCNS

No wrinkles or creases

You had to make damn sure your bed was made properly – no wrinkles or creases and the corners perfect. Your buttons, your ties, your shoes, the whole works had to be perfect for kit inspection. Everything they had issued you had to be out on your bed in a certain way, too. You had to be able to see your face in your shoes and my uniform was pressed to perfection; and, I was so good at it, I used to do a lot of the other girls' shirts and uniforms as well as my own.

You'd get up in the morning, shower, get into your uniform, make your bed and get over to breakfast within a certain time. Then as soon as you got out of there, you'd have to line up to parade back to the barracks. Then after about half an hour we'd have to get out to the parade square and there we'd be from about eight o'clock till noon, drilling, marching, that was the Army way. Then in the afternoons, during this six weeks we'd learn all about gas masks and first aid and then there were the needles . . . We all had to have our *needles* and they gave them to us all at once. It was sort of like sticking a bunch of pigs, I thought. *Next! Next!* That's what I remember. Some would pass out, of course. Then there was more on VD, and then we'd have to take turns in the mess halls. Some days you'd have pots and pans coming out of your ears and other days you'd be peeling all the vegetables, and another day you'd be helping the cook. Everybody had turns.

Former member, CWAC

An RCAF Christmas on the station (location unidentified).

Naked, but at attention, as required

During their training, one of my duties was to take care of people if they were tight coming in at night and if they misbehaved, we'd run them, which meant they'd be charged and they'd have to come up before the captain the next day.

We were trained that we were to behave as if we were on board a ship and the regulators carried a ship's bosun pipe with them on their rounds with the officer of the day and her entourage, as she inspected the ship – even the heads (toilets). The minute the pipe sounded "Still for Rounds," everyone would have to stand to attention as we passed through . . . even to the point of no return, where one kid stepped out of the shower, stark naked – but standing to attention as required.

Former member, WRCNS

Snow on my pillow

The camp was bleak and cheerless. Great huge huts covered in tar paper.

The men had just moved out that morning and our company of girls arrived for training at noon, amidst a howling snowstorm. Our huts were heated with round coal stoves which were a trial to keep going and those on night fire duty often let them go out. Many times I woke up to find snow on my pillow and my wash cloth frozen to my bunk . . . And, there was just no privacy, even to go to the bathroom, as at that stage they hadn't had time to put doors on the toilets. It was difficult to adjust to those circumstances, but there was a job to be done. After all, our brothers and boyfriends were overseas and they needed all the back-up power they could get. After a while, a great spirit of comradeship developed, since we'd all had to put up with those chilling workouts on that huge drill square and sat through all those lectures together. We got used to many different personalities and each of our lives was enriched by the many different types of Canadians that we came in contact with in Basic.

Former member, CWAC

A mixed bag

Nothing anyone could have told me would have really prepared me for all the various types I'd encounter in the service. There was one woman who happened to be beside me when we were all learning to march, back and forth all around the drill hall. And I, being tall, was in the last rank and suddenly this character next to me says, "Ain't it a bugger when you don't know your left foot from your right?" It almost unhinged me on the spot. And language . . . that was certainly one of the shocks to me, the free use of what my mother referred to as "coarse language." I guess I knew all the four-letter words, alright, but I'd never heard them used as a matter of course. and I have to admit I was using quite a few of them myself by the time 1945 came along.

Former member, RCAF (WD)

Just let them lie there

Basic Training was hilarious. It was the dead of winter. We'd march for hours and stand at attention for hours and people started flaking out all over the place. If it happened to be someone right next to you, you couldn't try to pick them up or anything, you just had to let them lie there. We had to take fire drill and picket duty . . . this was about once a week . . . in shifts. But your shift changed each time and it didn't matter which shift you were on – even the night shift had to go on parade the next day. One time, I guess a bunch of us had all been out the night before and had hangovers, because we decided to go on sick parade. Well, the medical officer went to our officer and she told her there wasn't a thing wrong with us except that we were all hung over, so our whole weekend was spent scrubbing the damn old garage with mops and these little wee brooms.

Former member, CWAC

Running like a rabbit

We had one girl in Galt who was extra fond of throwing back the drinks, and the tavern would call us and say, "We've got a girl here who needs to be taken home." And then we'd go off and fetch her in the panel truck. When we got there, we went in and found her and told her we thought it was time she came home, and then we put her in the back of the truck. Well, the driver forgot to lock the door and before we knew it, she was out of the truck and running like a rabbit down the main street, with the two of us, myself and the driver, trying to catch up with her. If she hadn't had so much to drink, she might have outrun us, but finally we got her back into the truck . . . only this time the door was definitely locked. By the time we got her back to *Conestoga*, she was pretty wild and the duty officer called the medical officer right away to give her a shot to calm her down. Four people had to hold her down – one on each arm and leg, even though she was just a little bit of a thing. But it all seemed to be a bit unnecessary. In fact, you'd wonder whether or not the duty officer would have subjected her to all that if she hadn't known she was part Indian.

Former member, WRCNS

Old soldiers standing at rigid attention

Our first route march came after we had been in training for three weeks; we were to act as escort for the graduating basic squadron. It was a blazing hot day, but our ardour was dampened only by perspiration. (There was plenty of that.) When we got under way, we felt that we were squirting like city street-sprinkler units. We fell in, feeling very important.

In front of us was the band; behind us was a station wagon to pick up the fallen. The corporal told us later that she held it against us that none of us fainted so that she could get a ride back in the wagon with the casualty.

The streets were crowded in spots with people who cheered or made sassy remarks. There were spatters of applause, but the most touching thing was the sight of old soldiers standing at rigid attention.

Former member, RCAF (WD)

National Archives of Canada, PA-128227

CWAC personnel en route to Washington, D.C., from Ottawa, June 9, 1942.

Graduation . . . simple!

In spite of our deeply rooted conviction that our training would *never* be over, the day of our graduation dawned bright and fair. (Actually it was bleak and chill.) All morning we were to rehearse for the important ceremony, which, with our final route march, was to launch us upon the warring world.

There was an honour certificate awarded to the airwoman in each "trade" graduating with the highest degree of proficiency as judged by her marks in her final examination, her weekly tests, her practical work (such as typing or driving), her drill, her deportment. Four trades were represented that day so four girls would be called out of line to be presented with honour certificates. The parade square was marked out with dear little coloured flags for the march-past, and already camp chairs were being set up where our guests of the afternoon could sit and shiver. It was very impressive . . . exciting.

We were lined up as usual and stood at ease. Our drill sergeant announced that he would be the CO [commanding officer] and call out the names of girls who would act as honour students. Each, as her name was called, was to answer "Sir," come quickly up to the station sergeant major, who would be playing the part of the visiting officer, stop two paces in front of him, salute, take a pace forward, accept the certificate in the left hand, be shaken hands with in the right, step back, salute, about turn, return to her place in line, take a dressing, etc. Simple!

Former member, RCAF (WD)

Reporting out

Once the training was over and we graduated from the transport, everyone got their orders to report to different places. Some were staying in Kitchener, some were coming to Toronto, some were going out West, some were going down East or to Kingston. Then you were almost on the next train out. They didn't waste any time. Once most of the people had gone, there weren't enough of us to keep the pot-bellied stoves going. We damn near froze to death, I can tell you. We were sleeping with mattresses on top of us to try to keep warm. *Cold!* I'll never forget it!

Former member, CWAC

Culling out the oddballs

Once we were finished with Basic Training, most of the real oddballs had been culled out. Not necessarily the ones that might get into mischief, but the misfits, the ones who'd never make it.

Former member, WRCNS

All we knew was that we were itchy

We all had to be inspected for head lice, and *crabs*, too, I might add. Another girl and I actually got them. I guess we were pretty naive, because we didn't know what they were. All we knew was that we were itchy, so we finally had to go to the medical centre and get it looked after.

Former member, CWAC

Map-reading in a bar

During training we'd go map-reading way out in the country, and there was one instructor we'd always try to get because we could be almost certain we'd get lost and end up in a bar somewhere. And we'd come back afterwards and she'd give us high marks. But one time we all got reported and then we had to scrub down the old garage. I guess it must have been a civilian that saw the army truck outside the bar and maybe we got a little loud . . . anyway, we had to pay for our fun.

Former member, CWAC

Courtesy A.F. Gasbarini, private collection

Group of RCAF (WD)s temporarily adopt some pups while visiting Camp Petawawa, Ont., 1944.

Eighty questions in thirty minutes

My trade was assigned when I went in. Apparently they were looking for meteorological observers and I'd passed one of those classification tests you had to do when you went in. It was one of those things where you had to answer about eighty questions in thirty minutes or something. Anyway, I guess I must have done well, because the next thing I knew, I'd been assigned for training as a met observer. Fortunately they didn't want cooks or messwomen at the time, because I think it was probably as much of a lottery as that.

Former member, RCAF (WD)

"Leftenant" – British pronunciation

I remember the first or second week of Basic Training, I felt quite homesick – being an American, maybe more so than most – and I wondered if I had made the right decision. All of the Americans were called to the lieutenant's quarters (I still think "leftenant" – British pronunciation) and I thought cheerfully that perhaps they had decided to discharge all of us. They were only taking photographs, however.

Former member, CWAC

Courtesy Barbara A. Cole, private collection

CWAC members enjoy a sing-along during Basic Training at Kitchener, Ont., October 1943.

I heard my first bagpipes

After Basic Training, I spent a short period of time in Toronto. My main memory of that is of parading down Yonge Street in a greatcoat which was much too long, while the snow was falling. It was only late September or early October but the snow was coming down hard and I heard my first bagpipes. Then I was sent to Montreal for a few months. My high school French was completely useless, but very few of the English-speaking people I met spoke French at all, while virtually all of the French-speaking people with any formal education at all spoke at least some English, and many were quite fluent. But they were expected to speak English. That was the prevailing attitude.

Former member, CWAC

Those darn typewriter keys

From Basic Training at Vermilion, I went to Winnipeg on a clerk's course. We marched from the barracks – a big house on the river – to a school, every afternoon after the children were finished. I often couldn't get to sleep at night thinking of those darn typewriter keys.

Former member, CWAC

Toast and marmalade three times daily

We were a class of twenty-six girls attending Central High School of Commerce and some of us "lived out" at Rochdale House on Spadina Avenue, chaperoned by a senior NCO. My Toronto memories included being late for afternoon classes because of going to see the "Happy Gang" from noon until one o'clock. I remember visiting Sunnyside on Saturday nights; spending weekends with my aunt who spent her summers on Centre Island; Casa Loma, the service canteen, walks along Yonge Street and College Street; visits to Borden's Dairy for banana splits, blueberry pie and ice cream after payday; quick trips at noon for toast and marmalade at Rochdale House before payday. I could never seem to make my pay stretch. I had assigned $20 monthly home to my mother, and always managed to eat well at the school cafeteria the first week after payday, but the second week my diet of toast and marmalade three times daily grew wearisome. There were the drill periods at Central High each afternoon, at which time I was nicknamed "Smiley" by our drill corporal. That name has stuck for forty years. We graduated in late October of 1943, and though I begged for a posting to Calgary and home, it was not to be. At least, not for a while.

Former member, CWAC

No malingerers, please

Right from the start in Basic Training it was made very clear that the Navy didn't want malingerers. We were told in no uncertain terms, "If you're one of those people who needs to take off one or two days every time you menstruate . . . you might as well pack it in right now! We don't want you running to the medical officer complaining about cramps."

Former officer, WRCNS

It was unbelievably ghastly

We started at 6 a.m. It was unbelievably ghastly. They wanted to weed out the weaklings. By the end of the first two or three days, or at most by the end of the first week, most of them had left. They couldn't take it. In those days, women weren't used to "physical conditioning" of that sort.

Former member, CWAC

A cook is not a dietician

(v) Once again may it be stressed to Recruiting Officers that the final

National Archives of Canada, PA-128252

Cpl. Patricia Johnson, CWAC, working in the kitchen of Kildare Barracks, Ottawa, Ont., April 1944.

decision as to trade rests entirely with the Selection Board, who consider the preferences of the Trainee together with her qualifications and the trades open at the time.

(vi) When Recruits are enlisted as Cooks they have no opportunity of appearing before the Selection Board to remuster to another trade. There have been several instances lately of recruits enlisting as cooks, and being told by the Recruiting Officer that something might be done at the Manning Depot to get them into another trade. Also, a cook is not a dietician as some of them have been led to suppose.

RCAF (W.D.) Memo to:
Secretary of National Defence for Air
June, 1943

Hostesses

A lot of the girls that enlisted were told that they'd be given jobs that they never got . . . or the job was made to sound quite different than it was. People who were told that they could be stewards, because towards the end of the war that was almost the only job available, were given the impression that they'd be sort of hostesses in the officers' mess – little knowing that they'd have to clean up all ungodly kinds of mess after all the parties night after night. Eventually, it really got to some of them. One of them got so depressed by it that she was threatening to commit suicide and her friends were taking turns sitting up with her to make sure she didn't do something foolish like jump out of the window.

So, the doctor examined her. Nothing wrong with her chest, no cold or anything – back on duty. This happened a number of times and the doctor kept saying, "There's nothing wrong with you." Finally, she came back from seeing the doctor and said that if anything happened to her, not under any circumstances should her mother be told because she had had a brother who had gone crazy, and that if they sent her home for being crazy, it would be too much for her mother. Finally then, they decided to take her seriously and she was sent down to Ste. Anne de Bellevue where they had a home for people with mental disorders. She was there for about a year and a half. When she was discharged as being mentally and physically fit, what did they do but send her straight home, against her wishes; and two weeks later, she committed suicide.

Former member, WRCNS

None of it seemed to apply to me
After I'd been in England for a while, I was sent to officer training school. It was run by the British ATS and there were twelve Canadians. First we had to write an exam set by Canadians. Forty-five of us wrote the exam, and then twelve of us got through that and went before a selection board plus two days of every imaginable kind of test. We were all convinced we'd failed. They were looking for people who could react quickly and sensibly, and who had a sense of responsibility . . . and none of it seemed to apply to me, particularly. To my great surprise, I managed to get through.

Former officer, CWAC

Luckily, I had a good memory
I'd never worked in my life. I guess you could call me privileged. I'd been living in Europe from the age of fourteen till I was twenty-one, so I was fit for nothing and didn't really know much about anything that had to do with work. When I got to Trenton, they started talking about vouchers and

RCAF (WD) personnel perform semaphore drill at Wireless School, Montreal, Que.

bills of lading and I didn't know what in heaven's name they were even talking about. It was awful! Luckily, I had a good memory and managed to get through the examinations; and off I went to my first job.

Former member, RCAF (WD)

Just like joining the Foreign Legion

When we got our uniforms, we had to ship all our civilian clothes home, it was just like joining the Foreign Legion, cutting all ties with the past. We packed them all up in cartons and took them down to be shipped and then came back to the barracks and cried a lot. Then we felt they really had us . . . When you signed up and read on the paper "For the Duration" . . . I started thinking of things like the Hundred Years' War. It shook me quite a lot.

Former member, RCAF (WD)

Canadian Forces Photographic Unit, DND, PL-12062

Molly Lamb Bobak, *Outside Barracks, Canadian Army Trades School,* ca. 1943.

FOUR

All in Together, Girls

FOR ENLISTED WOMEN (OTHER RANKS), communal living was a basic fact of life in uniform. While officers may have had more commodious lodgings, a greater degree of privacy, and fewer restrictions in their day-to-day existence, they were also the "responsible parties" and as such probably deserved a modicum of comfort to compensate for the inherent strains and pressures of leadership. The exigencies of wartime made temporary, ill-equipped quarters the rule rather than the exception. If the cubicles in the WCs had no doors when servicewomen first occupied new quarters, this was remedied . . . sooner or later. Or if insulation in the walls was non-existent, cracks were stuffed with newspapers until something more permanent could be done about it. If the mattresses were Posturepedic rejects more closely resembling a hammock, it was just another of service life's little inconveniences.

Besides, it was permissible to add homey touches such as bouquets of wild flowers here and there. Pin-ups of Clark Gable, Alan Ladd, and Robert Taylor (among others) also helped to brighten otherwise bleak surroundings, as well as photos of family and sweethearts, banners, insignia, and any number of other items that might enhance the decor slightly.

The official RCAF description of airwomen's accommodation read:

Airwomen occupy barrack blocks like those of airmen . . . two dormitory wings joined by ablutions rooms and laundry. The wings contain double-decker bunks; a bedroom with shower being provided for the sergeant in one wing, a double room for the two corporals in the other. Officers have their own quarters in a small bungalow of their own . . . two bedrooms, bathroom, living-room and hall with kitchenette . . . The airwomen's recreation centre consists of a dry canteen (no alcoholic beverages), a games room, reading room, library and sitting room. The blocks are designed to accommodate 68 airwomen in each wing, each having an upper or lower bed, a locker and space for hanging clothes.[1]

And on the subject of "messing":

Airwomen eat in the airmen's mess, where food is served cafeteria fashion, and tables are reserved for their use. Corporals have their own table there or eat in the NCOs' mess, the sergeant in the Sergeants' Mess. Officers eat in the Officers' Mess.[2]

"Messing" – the preparation and presentation of food for the uniformed masses – was another target for internal criticism. And here again, a certain basic resignation had to be acquired. For cooks, working conditions were often less than perfect. Some kinds of food were more available than others or more economical to serve. Some foods were in short supply, and indeed, some cooks were more dedicated or imaginative than others. It was the luck of the draw, but every attempt was made to provide meals that were at least nutritionally balanced:

It is the duty of the medical officer to give instruction in the value of health producing, nutritionally balanced meals, properly prepared from fresh foods. It is also the duty of the medical officer to see that the food is prepared and served in an attractive way and eaten in pleasant surroundings so that appetites are stimulated and nutrition maintained by balanced Army meals, rather than by consumption of nutritionally poor foods bought in canteens and elsewhere. Informal discussions on nutrition should frequently take place with cooks, messing officers, and quartermasters. Formal lectures on nutrition should be given at least once in each six weeks, to all officers and other ranks, and all personnel should be made conversant with their food entitlements as laid down in the scale of rations.[3]

Air Minister C.G. Power chats with WD clerk accountants, leading airwomen J. Hamlet of Fort William, Ont., and E.B. McClymont of Newmarket, Ont., in RCAF mess hall.

Undoubtedly some of the complaints levelled at those responsible for "messing" were justified, but consistency of quality was next to impossible. Circumstances were, after all, scarcely ideal for the production of gourmet meals three times a day. That the food should be nourishing and prepared under hygienic conditions was a given, but beyond that it was more or less a matter of chance, rather than choice . . .

CWAC policy on messing was similar to that of the Air Force:

It is not intended that the CWAC will mess indiscriminately with the men. Certain tables will be set aside for them in the men's messes. The women will not march to their meals. A separate entrance will be made in the mess hall . . . This system has been in use for some time by the RCAF (W.D.) and is working satisfactorily in every respect.[4]

Inspections, parades, marching, and drill were all part of the military package and not affected by scarcities of any sort. Regular three- to ten-mile route marches were routine on most stations and bases. Unfortunately, service walking shoes or Oxfords were not always a perfect fit and the aftermath of a good brisk route march was usually an epidemic of corns, bunions, and blisters to serve as fond reminders of yet another shared experience in uniform. In late 1942 Maj.-Gen. Jean Knox of the British ATS visited Canada, and during one of the many meetings held during her stay the subject of route marches was discussed at some length. According to the minutes of this particular meeting, Major-General Knox considered a route march of over three miles to be both unnecessary and dangerous to health. She also pointed out that in England some difficulty had been experienced in that a recruit used to wearing high-heeled shoes was frequently troubled by sore feet, due to the change to low heels and an increased amount of walking. This, in turn, increased the need for shoes of a larger size to accommodate the expansion of the feet. One of the Canadian brass present suggested that this problem could be solved by issuing insoles with shoes to be worn until such time as the foot enlarged and the insole was no longer necessary; a practical suggestion, but, Major-General Knox pointed out that even then there would be considerable foot trouble. In other words, she was not an advocate of lengthy route marches, regardless of the footgear that might be available.[5]

Nor was she alone in her views on the subject. The necessity of subjecting essentially non-masochistic women to this sort of gruelling exercise in endurance escaped many people. Would any of these women ever need to cover long distances on foot in the service of their country? Did they, in fact, require the disciplined ask-no-questions type of pre-combat training and conditioning that servicemen had to receive if they were to be effective in battle? At the time, of course, there were more urgent concerns and the simplest way of dealing with the female fact in uniform was to make use of the existing models with very minor modifications.

But whether it was ill-fitting shoes or clothing in general, the complaints department was under continual assault on a number of counts. Trench coats, for instance, did not always keep out the rain and were of poor quality. Zippers did not zip properly. Uniforms, if they were to look smart, required periodic alterations. Underwear and girdles were not kept in stock by "stores" as a convenience and the three-dollar quarterly underclothing allowance was inadequate. Under the indignant barrage of wrongs that required affirmative action, those responsible must have found it very difficult to maintain a stiff upper lip.

But for most servicewomen, it was the excessive and often unreasonable rules and regimentation that got them down. Especially when they encountered officers who, allowing their authority to go to their heads, gave no quarter. One could consider oneself extremely fortunate if one happened to be placed under the command of an individual who possessed equal measures of humour and humanity.

Religion, too, had its place in the life of a woman in uniform. Not that everyone who enlisted was fervently or devoutly religious; certainly not the volunteer who, when asked what her religion was, responded by asking what religion there was a shortage of – Baptists, perhaps? or Seventh-Day Adventists?

Essentially, religion was considered a personal matter, but Sunday services and church parades, by virtue of tradition, were an aspect of the military experience shared by everyone in the services, male or female. Chaplains assigned to various bases were instructed to hold a weekly "padre's hour" for the information and guidance of anyone who chose to attend.

Take the following directive, for example:

Each hour should consist primarily of a debate on a specific problem. The debate should be opened by the Chaplain who will speak briefly with the object of stimulating interest and thought. After that the Chaplain will act as chairman of the debate and encourage the women to do most of the talking, directing it on sound lines in accordance with true Christian principles.

In choosing the matter which will form the subject of discussion, Chaplains will consider the type of women with whom they have to deal. Audiences will be mixed, containing some women who have intense religious convictions and others with none at all. There will even be found women who have had no religious teaching whatever. It is important, therefore, that in order to stimulate the interest of these women, the basis of discussion be something practical which touches every woman in her daily life – some problem with which she is constantly confronted.[6]

Servicewomen of the Jewish faith were granted leave, subject to change if necessary, for observance of religious holidays and were also given sufficient time to reach a place of worship by sunset of the previous day, in accordance with Jewish custom.

Canadian Forces Photographic Unit, DND, PL-33156

Members of the RCAF HQ softball team watch men's final game in Edinburgh.

Private collection

WRCNS Dominion Day Regatta 1945 (location unknown).

For many women, participation in team sports after hours seems to have provided a welcome change from the daily routine. It helped to break up the monotony of an otherwise regulated life and probably served as a harmless and healthy outlet for energies that might otherwise have been misspent . . . in the bushes, or wherever else trouble might be found.

RECREATIONAL ACTIVITIES:
Organized sports play an important part in station life. Softball, badminton, tennis, hockey, are included, with swimming where available, supervised picnics, and hiking. Ping-pong is also played, and time allotted to physical training. Concerts, choral singing and amateur theatricals are also popular, as are the station dances which are held from time to time.[7]

The problem of sex and its by-products, venereal disease and pregnancy, caused those in charge of dealing with such matters more than their share of headaches. When sex reared its ugly head, whether conjugal, extramarital, or just plain fooling around – whatever its kind or intensity – it was difficult to ignore. In fact, it created untold problems, of which VD was only one of a multitude. From the servicewoman's standpoint, pregnancy was an instant ticket back to civilian life. Discharges were granted on medical grounds or for compassionate reasons. The CWAC form for medical officers "in charge of personnel (other than married women) who became pregnant" posed some awkward questions of a highly personal nature:

Were you pregnant before enlistment?   Yes?   No?

If so, how long?

How far were you from your home town?

Were quarters provided in barracks?   Yes?   No?

Were you on subsistence in your own
home? A private home? A boarding house?
A hostel? A hotel?

Are you engaged?   Yes?   No?

Do you consider yourself engaged? Yes? No?

Do you take part in organized recreation
or sports? Yes? No?

Did you receive instructions on
sex and hygiene? Yes? No? by whom?

How long had you known the putative father?

Had you been drinking? Yes? No? [8]

These and other "pro forma" papers were to be returned to NDHQ with monthly reports of pregnancy and VD occurring in each military district. Once the form had been filled in and sent off, it was not long before the woman in question received a "Notice of Termination of Service." Officers could relinquish their appointments "at the pleasure of the Minister" and other ranks could "apply to obtain a discharge on account of (a) marriage or (b) compassionate grounds" ... with the additional instruction that: "Pregnancy is a cause for retirement or discharge on Medical grounds."[9]

The Air Force, within a year of commencing female enlistment, was facing problems similar to those encountered by the CWAC:

Airwomen discharged for pregnancy
1.   The future of airwomen discharged for pregnancy is a matter for concern and the decision with regard to procedure will be promulgated in due course. A women's committee is being set up under the auspices of the Special Committee on Reconstruction and Re-establishment and this committee will make recommendations.
2.   In the meantime, the Director of the Social Welfare Committee is willing to advise regarding getting help for individual cases during the period of pregnancy and for care of the child, et cetera. W.D. Administrative Officers on Stations should notify the W.D. Officer at Commands, confidentially, of the name, home address and circumstances of the airwoman concerned, and the W.D. Officer at Command should notify the Senior W.D. Officer, A.M.P. Division. She will consult the Director of the Social Welfare Council and communicate with the W.D. Officer at Command.[10]

On rare occasions the stork arrived unexpectedly, before discharge could be effected. When this occurred, the resulting consternation was considerable for all concerned, but the end result was the same as if there had been prior notification. The expectant (or new) mother was granted a speedy discharge, usually within seven to ten days.

It was impressed upon all commanding officers, however, that the utmost confidentiality should be maintained, and that all possible steps should be taken to ensure the future welfare of the mother and child upon her release from the service in terms of hospitalization and housing before and after the blessed event. Whether this confidentiality was considered essential for humanitarian reasons or whether the concern was based on possible damage to the public image of the services is a matter open to conjecture.[11]

Warnings on the subject of abortions were also issued to all officers in the WD.

Abortions that are artificially induced are illegal. They are also dangerous. The second chief cause of death in Ontario of women between 15 and 40 years of age is maternity, and nearly half these deaths are associated with septic abortions.[12]

Aside from pregnancy, the principal grounds for discharge in all three services were "psychoneurotic illness or disorders" and "general unsuitability" – a classification which could cover a multiplicity of sins. Since each service had its own "code," comparisons are difficult; however, the severity of the problems in the women's services is indicated by the figures for annual number of servicewomen discharged accumulated by military historians after the war.[13]

	WRCNS	CWAC	RCAF (WD)
1941	–	40	6
1942	7	502	334
1943	233	2,258	1,058
1944	536	3,310	2,263
1945	307	1,121	2,103

The mental stability and emotional welfare of their personnel was of great concern to all the services, and each, in its own fashion, attempted to grapple with the inevitable problems of dealing with large numbers of people living at close quarters. In the considered opinion of Army psychiatrists, it was women who were more prone to "situational problems."

(a) <u>Situational Problems</u> – Emotional disturbances due to relatively minor situational difficulties arise more frequently among women than among men. This is particularly apt to occur when some personal problem or worry is aggravated by a feeling of resentment against the individual's allocation. Other factors are boredom, lack of suitable recreation, fatigue, etc. Many of these temporary emotional disturbances, with prompt and energetic treatment, subside without any need for further action.

The R.M.O. can, with the help of such officers as the Company Commander, Army Examiner and the Welfare Officer, attempt to assess and correct the situation producing the emotional upset. Treatment should include – first, a full discussion of the problem, with plenty of encouragement and reassurance; and then, if necessary, reallocation to other duties, and reposting to another area should be arranged. In some of these individuals, a period of leave is very beneficial.[14]

Women of a more truly eccentric temperament, however, posed a more serious problem.

(b) <u>Personality Problems</u> – A number of C.W.A.C. personnel are meeting difficulties because of minor eccentricities of temperament or personality. In these cases, it is not the situation primarily that is causing the difficulty. Those types of individuals are frequently apt to create friction and discord in almost any situation. While, strictly speaking, they are temperamentally unstable, the condition hardly warrants the diagnosis of a full-blown psychiatric disability.

These individuals usually should be referred to the Army Psychiatrist for examination and treatment. They should be diagnosed as Temperamental Instability. Their allocation is most important. They should *not* be placed under conditions of strain or tension. If the symptoms persist after reasonable therapeutic measures have been carried out and the individual remains unsuitable for service, consideration should be given to an administrative discharge.[15]

Homosexuality appears to have been a relatively minor cause of concern. There were definitely occasions when the issue had to be addressed and acted upon appropriately, but its incidence appears to have been limited or else ignored. It is difficult to know the exact extent of this particular sexual proclivity, but official pronouncements on the matter indicate that its existence was at least recognized, if not condoned.

The Army's evaluation of "Homosexualism" (*sic*) was that this condition was fairly rare in women. However, these words of caution were passed on:

> When there are large groups of women all living together, it [lesbianism] must be watched for ALWAYS, and, if a case does occur, it should be looked on as a medical problem, not a moral one.[16]

Nor did it appear to be causing the Air Force problems of any magnitude:

> Homosexuality has not been a problem in the W.D. There have been occasional cases which were investigated and a discharge effected on those in whom a neuropsychiatrist confirmed the diagnosis. However, the number has been negligible.[17]

As for that other abnormal condition "associated with the psychological aspect of reproduction" (an Army physician's terminology), "Masturbation among women is not as common as it is among men . . . It does not lead to mental illness, nor are many of the ideas associated with it true." No doubt this helped allay the fears of those who had been under the impression that their hands might turn green.[18]

When word of these discharges seeped out, as it inevitably did, it only helped to add fuel to the fire of public opposition to the concept of women in uniform. Perhaps the experience of one Women's Army Corps member was an isolated indication of public antipathy, but on a personal level it had a rather shattering effect. While travelling as a passenger on a crowded bus, she offered her seat to an elderly woman standing in front of her. The offer was rejected out of hand, and she was told in no uncertain terms that it was infinitely preferable to stand than to accept a seat from a camp follower in uniform.

The public perception of servicewomen's morality was clearly removed from reality, but it was an entrenched position nonetheless. In the public opinion survey conducted in 1943 by Elliott Haynes Ltd. of Toronto and Montreal, sundry comments reflect a virulent prejudice against the presence of women in the armed forces:

The personnel of CWAC is recruited preferably among ladies of easy virtue. (Montreal, September 1942)

CWAC and airwomen are now being supplied with prophylactics by their medical officers for the prevention of V.D. (Barrie, Ontario, October 1942)

Conditions in camps where girls are stationed are bad and men are allowed to mix with the girls. In some camps – east of Winnipeg – when the lights are turned on, girls are not only on the beds but under the beds of soldiers and airmen. (Winnipeg, December 1942)

I was thinking of renting my spare room, when I was warned not to take a member of the CWAC because they all have syphilis. (Westmount, Que., December 1942)

The government has set aside a special building for Air Force and Army women to give birth to their illegitimate children. (Winnipeg, December 1942)

The first W.D.s to join were girls from the Red Light Districts, so you can see there is much in what people say. For instance, in one case, thirty-seven CWACs landed at Esquimalt and twenty-eight were pregnant. (Victoria, B.C., December 1942)

Innovation of any sort is always bound to create suspicion and certainly the women who enlisted in Canada's armed forces were the objects of a good deal of scepticism from within and without. They had demonstrated that they could indeed work "shoulder to shoulder" with men, but the slogan had connotations that could be interpreted in a negative sense. Random stories of servicewomen's promiscuity were often the direct result of exemplary moral standards. It was not uncommon for a disgruntled swain, when given the "brush-off," to take revenge by attempting to blacken the character of servicewomen in general.

Regrettably, too, the young and beautiful prototypes selected by public relations officials to personify feminine pulchritude in uniform often did more harm than good. Civilian women with husbands in uniform were less than charmed; nor were those women in the service upon whom nature had smiled less kindly entirely delighted with the image being projected – an image far removed from what they saw in the mirror every morning.

A sense of humour seems to have been a prerequisite for the "shared experience" of communal living. Generally, people came to accept that there were certain things they would have to bear, so they might as well try to grin while they were at it. Co-existence with up to 140 other women in a barracks was not most people's idea of paradise. In the enlistment process, humour, or the lack of it, was not something that could be tested or measured. And if it was dormant in the beginning, it was only a matter of weeks before it surfaced. Not everyone found the same things amusing or even fun, but relatively few were loners, choosing to isolate themselves, psychologically if not physically, from their bunk mates. For the most part, once the initial shock had worn off, most women adapted to communal living with relative ease. They found friends with similar interests, formed cliques or groups, and developed their own particular loyalties. In short, they made the best of things. They did not, however, totally conform to accepted military practice. Most women, in fact, immediately set out to find new and inventive ways of getting around the rules and restrictive regulations which were meant to keep them in check, if not "in their place."

A degree of doubt about a woman's place began to filter into what had previously been rarefied air. No one, male or female, was quite as sure about it as he or she had been, once upon a time, when women other than nurses would never have been dreamt of as an integral part of His Majesty's Canadian Armed Forces. But there was a war to be won in the meantime, and women in uniform could certainly do their bit.

Notebook

Routine:

Routine of the station, except for cooks and those working on special shifts, begins with reveille at 6, breakfast at 7. The airwoman must have her shoes and brass buttons shined, her bed made, her possessions tidily stowed before inspection and morning parade, which is at 8. Work commences after that and continues till dinner time, at 12. Working parade (afternoon roll-call) is at 1:15, after which work is resumed till 5. Supper is served then, with lights out at 10:30.

RCAF (W.D.) Bulletin, 1942

National Archives of Canada, PA-141007

Unidentified member of CWAC carrying a respirator, August 1943.

Women not wanted

On that station, the CO didn't want women. He hated the whole idea . . . and they did absolutely nothing for us. There was no heat in the barracks. Nobody ever came to meet us. We had to carry our stuff for miles up to the barracks, and it was the dead of winter. But we stuck it out.

Former member, RCAF (WD)

There was no yardstick

So many of us had never been up against anything like this before. It was like a chunk out of my life that had no connection with anything that happened before or afterwards. In the service, there was no yardstick . . . You were all sharing the same quarters, eating the same food, wearing the same uniform. It was a great leveller.

Former member, RCAF (WD)

It did us all good

We certainly had people from one coast to the other, and that was a help in a way, having everyone from all over the map like that. Cliques or groups of people with similar interests, or the same sense of mischief or whatever, did form, but still, you learned to live with every imaginable kind of person, from every possible walk of life . . . and it did us all good.

Former member, RCAF (WD)

With my curlers frozen in my hair

We were in huts that the Army had been in and you could actually see daylight through the cracks. We used to have to go out early in the morning and split wood and carry it in to keep the pot-bellied stoves going, or I think we would have all frozen to death. One time, I was carrying this armful of wood and I saw an officer coming. I dropped the whole thing and whipped up a salute. It was like second nature to us by then to salute an officer, no matter what!

At night, sometimes we'd get hungry, so we'd take bread from the mess hall and put a couple of pieces under our hats to get it out, and then toast it on a wire coat hanger over the stove in our hut.

Sometimes it got so cold that I'd sleep in my uniform; and, one night I remember waking up and finding my curlers frozen in my hair.

Former member, WRCNS

No better insulator than newspaper

One of my uncles who'd been in the First War told me (when I was complaining about the cold), that there was no better insulator than newspaper. So, taking his advice, I came back from home with a huge bundle of newspapers to put under my mattress. As it happened, shortly after this there was a big inspection and there we all were standing at attention with everything polished to the nines. As the CO came down the line, I saw him suddenly freeze and then look down. My first thought was, "I know I polished it last night. What could he be looking at?" Then I was commanded to step one pace forward and give an explanation. There were tattered shreds of newspaper hanging down from between the springs of my bunk. I guess as I'd been rolling over in the night, those springs were cutting into the newspapers like knives. And again I was put "on charge." I had to be confined to barracks for three days and scrub out toilets or wash windows or whatever.

Former member, RCAF (WD)

Canadian Forces Photographic Unit, DND, PL-24469

After a twenty-eight-week wireless course the first of seven potential RCAF (WD) signals officers leave No. 3 Wireless School, Winnipeg, Man., for six weeks' officers training at Trenton, Ont. (Left to right: Nell Ross, Vancouver, B.C.; Mary Gordon, Toronto, Ont.; Louise LeClair, North Rustico, P.E.I.; Betty Dowler, Pigeon Lake, Alta.; Dorothy Winter, Regina, Sask.; Patricia Annand, Truro, N.S. Not shown is Cadet Officer Alma Lauer, Rosthern, Sask.)

While somebody held a flashlight

During the winter, we'd be on parade at some ungodly hour in the morning and it would be pitch black. The sergeant would call the roll while somebody held a flashlight and some of our sleepy-headed friends would say to us, "Oh, just say 'Here,'" because in the dark you couldn't see anything. Sometimes I'd feel like Mel Blanc shouting out "Here" in so many different voices; and by the time my own turn came, I hardly knew how to answer. Of course, we'd do it in turn so it would work out.

Former member, RCAF (WD)

Glorious galoshes

We wore glorious galoshes called "glamour boots" with buckles. My problem always was that when they sized the flight for marching, the tallest would be either in the front or at the back – so that the little guys wouldn't be left trailing along behind. My stride must have been a bit longer than most, because I always seemed to be stepping on the heels of someone in front of me, and if they were wearing rubbers they would inevitably come off just as we were passing the reviewing stand, and then they'd be cursing me.

I'd always try to stand next to a friend of mine who used to faint quite a lot, because then I'd have to help her off the parade square. But we never managed it as often as I would have liked.

Former member, RCAF (WD)

Strength through joy

Physical fitness was not my idea of fun. And whoever designed those outfits we had to wear obviously had something against females, because they were without a doubt the worst-looking outfits in the world. They were appalling – battleship grey T-shirts and shorts that must have been cut out with an axe, because they didn't fit anywhere. Then we'd have to go on these terrible route marches. Our station commander was one of these strength-through-joy types.

Former member, RCAF (WD)

After a while, it didn't matter

For a while, the French Canadians were more or less to themselves, but after a while it didn't matter who you were, or what you were – we all mixed. I got invited down to Quebec for a weekend by one girl, and it was my first exposure to a French Canadian family. Of course, all of them spoke French and I was the one that felt like a fool. The parents really tried more to speak English to me than they tried to make me understand French. They really tried to make me feel right at home among them. To tell you the truth, though, I felt very uncomfortable, in spite of all their kindness. It was the language difference, mainly, I think.

Former member, CWAC

A wonderful sense of humour

After I became an officer, I had a roommate from Quebec City, and she was a marvellous person. Such a wonderful sense of humour, and I loved her voice – so musical. That's where I gained respect for the French Canadians . . . it was from her.

Former officer, CWAC

Out! Out!

I went into a store in Ste.-Hyacinthe, Quebec, to buy something or other, and before I could even open my mouth, the owner was shouting at us, "Out! Out! Out!" in French. I had never realized how much we were resented there, until that moment. Some of my friends told me they'd been pushed off the street – or had even been spat on. I never could understand why they were so against us, because it must have helped the town's economy to have the Navy there . . . The only other civilian contact we had was the Anglican minister at the church there. He used to get us the odd bottle of wine.

Former officer, WRCNS

Members . . . engaged in sedentary work

The advice is that the food being served is no more unsuitable for women than for male clerks and other members of the Army engaged in sedentary work. It is not feasible to have a separate and distinct issue of rations for the CWAC.

Memo to Minister of Defence Ralston
from the Inspector General for Western Canada
June 6, 1942

Crawling with cockroaches

In Halifax it was unbelievable. You got a clean sheet every two months, and when we were on the midnight shift we'd go up for our meals and the dining room would be pitch black, because the cooks were all back in the kitchen. The bread was pre-cut, covered with a clean white cloth, one of us would go to the light switch, while the rest of us would go to the counter where the bread was standing. As the light went on, we'd whip off the white cloths and the bread would be crawling with cockroaches. As soon as the light was switched on they just vanished – as if into thin air – but nobody was very anxious to help themselves to bread, I can tell you!

Former member, WRCNS

American wonder dishes

We went through a period when somebody decided that if the American armed forces could eat off stainless steel trays that were divided into little sections, why couldn't we? It would cut down on the dishwashing, etc. So you'd be handed one of these plates, and I guess it was all beyond the poor

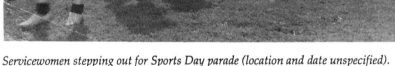

Servicewomen stepping out for Sports Day parade (location and date unspecified).

people who were trying to dish it out, because the chocolate sauce would be on the meat and the gravy would be on the ice cream and that would slop over onto the meat or the vegetables. After three weeks of all this, they gave up on these American "wonder dishes" and went back to the good old white stuff.

As for the *coffee* . . . I think they started the urns in 1939 and hadn't cleaned them out since. It went well with the uncooked bacon and over-cooked eggs. *Saltpetre* – no wonder we were all so tranquil. You could taste it unmistakably in the juice, and it was supposed to keep your sexual impulses in rein. It wasn't totally effective, I'm afraid. People's urges were stronger than the saltpetre!

Maybe it was the saltpetre, but I think most of us just took it for granted that there were certain things we had to do and put up with and we just accepted our situation. There were certain rules laid down for us. Not that we obeyed them all, but if you broke them, you knew the consequences of getting caught.

Former member, RCAF (WD)

Having been to boarding school helped

Maybe it was because I'd been through McGill, but a lot of the rules and regulations seemed so ridiculous and childish at that point. Accepting the silliness of certain aspects of this kind of life was pretty difficult for some of us. Having been to boarding school helped a little, except there, everyone had come from more or less the same background, whereas in the Air Force it was really a very mixed bag. Still, I guess having got used to a certain degree of regimentation and generally a fairly restricted kind of life, it was at least some kind of preparation for what lay ahead.

Former officer, RCAF (WD)

She'd be ticked off about it

In the beginning, among some of the fellows, there was a general attitude of resentment. They'd never really say anything; but it was irritating that an airman could do something, but if an airwoman did the same thing she'd be ticked off about it.

Former member, RCAF (WD)

You were going to come out second best

It was a special feeling. It wasn't like a job where you could say, "This bores me silly," or, "There's no challenge, I'm going to leave." In the Air Force there was no such thing. You were there for the duration and this got us all down sometimes, as I'm sure it did the men, too. Once you got used to it – resigned to it – it wasn't so bad, but a lot of us resented being ordered around. And there's no doubt about it, in the beginning particularly, many of the men in the service did resent the women. And there was no sense fighting back because you were going to come out second best . . . come what may.

And you got almost brainwashed about rank. If someone was a corporal or a sergeant, that was really something.

Former member, RCAF (WD)

I was always afraid of fire

I never slept very well in the barracks because I was always afraid of fire, and when I became an officer, this was one of my first concerns to make sure all the fire-fighting equipment was in order and all the exits clear, and so on . . .

I always preferred the upper bunk, because people used to hang their

I always preferred the upper bunk, because people used to hang their shirts up to dry and if you rolled over in the lower bunk you might very well get a wet shirt in your face.

Former officer, WRCNS

The music helped us to link up

There was a kind of a group of us who tended to spend our time together, mainly because we had common interests, I suppose, in what you might call the finer things of life. One girl had a lot of records, and we all gravitated to the music . . . It was the music that helped us to "link up." I suppose that, just naturally, you find the level of people that you have the most in common with, who think the same way.

Former member, RCAF (WD)

Pretty rough-and-tumble

I slept in a shift workers' barracks with all the cooks and messwomen and hospital attendants and some of them were pretty rough-and-tumble. Certainly it wasn't like anything I'd ever been used to. The shift workers' barracks was different, too, because there was always somebody asleep and somebody up, and in theory, anyway, you had to be very quiet . . . Curious, the things that stick in your mind. I remember that a lot of them always seemed to be eating oranges. Then they'd put their orange peels under the bunk and just leave them there, and the whole barracks used to have a sort of orange-peely smell. There were about eighty people – forty double bunks at least in each of the two sections of the building which was H-shaped with the ablution rooms in the cross-bar – the washrooms, two bathrooms, and a couple of showers (not very many for all those people, when you come to think of it) and then a row of johns and a laundry room.

Former member, RCAF (WD)

Even though you had your name on it

You'd go into the mess hall, hungry for their appalling food, hang up your greatcoat; eat; and then go back to where you thought you'd left your greatcoat. Even though you had your name in it, you'd try on about five before you'd get your own. I always seemed to pick ones that had sleeves that went to the elbow, because I was so tall and there would be my friend, who was small, in something that was trailing on the ground.

Former member, RCAF (WD)

National Archives of Canada, PA-128222

CWAC personnel sorting mail at base post office, Ottawa, Ont., November 23, 1943.

Stripped of all her badges

There were very strong deterrents as far as stealing was concerned. Not long after I arrived at Cornwallis, one girl was paraded out in front of everyone and stripped of all her badges, patches, and insignias because she'd stolen a brassiere, size 36, the property of Wren So-and-so, and one pair of black stockings, the property of Wren Somebody Else. Then she was dismissed from the service.

Former officer, WRCNS

National Archives of Canada, PA-129069

CWACs working on a motor, St. Anne's College, Val Cartier Camp, Que., April 1942.

I refused to go

When I was stationed in Dartmouth, there was a court-martial parade and I refused to go. Luckily I never got caught, but I just didn't approve of what they were going to do with her – taking all the buttons off her uniform and all her badges, and the whole public humiliation of it all, being marched off, stripped of everything, including your dignity. But that was the idea, I guess, to make it so dramatic that it would serve as a deterrent to the others.

Former member, WRCNS

Diamonds

Everyone was instructed that they were not to bring any valuables with them, but naturally there always has to be one, and in this case, it was a girl whose father was highly placed in Ottawa and who had her diamond ring and some pearls and watch all stolen. Well, as soon as Daddy found out, there was an all-out search. Nobody was to leave the building or use the toilets or move until every single Wren's kit had been gone through with a fine-toothed comb. Kotex pulled out of boxes, face cream jars held up to the light and so on; then after about two hours the search was called to a halt because someone had heard a toilet flushing. Sure enough, there was the diamond ring still in the bowl, but the pearls and the watch had disappeared down the drain. The next thing we knew they were digging up the drains behind the building to try and find the missing watch and necklace on Daddy's instructions.

Former member, WRCNS

Scrubbed twice every day

Some of the officers got very full of themselves and over-exercised their authority. We'd come back after doing a full day's work and then have to scrub the blasted floors when we got back, because the officers had decided that it was important for us to have extra duty. I later discovered that the floors in this particular building were scrubbed twice every day ... so we discovered ways of getting the floor cleaned with the least amount of effort in the shortest time possible. It almost seemed as if our own officers resented the hold that the male officers had over us during the day, so they had to exercise their own authority somehow.

Former officer, WRCNS

More than once we got stopped

The material in the officers' uniforms was different from ours, much finer, and we had to wear our pochette crossing over, whereas the officers could wear theirs on their shoulders. But, after we got off the "ship," we'd hang them on our shoulders. More than once we got stopped by a Wren officer for that, because they didn't like the idea of us trying to look like them.

Former member, WRCNS

Why should I do what she tells me?

We had to do whatever was expected of us. We had to do what we were told, that was all there was to it. No questions asked. Mind you, I don't think women take to orders as readily or as easily as men do. And indeed, I can remember people saying, "Why should I do what *she* tells me, for heaven's sake, she's only a corporal?" There were many people who found this aspect of being in the service very trying.

Former member, RCAF (WD)

The tribe

Despite higher pay, better uniforms and a number of other perks, I think women officers on flying stations had a pretty thin time of it. For one thing, there were so few of them, and life could be lonely since they weren't supposed to fraternize with other ranks. On an SFTS [Service Flight Training School] there might be two women officers in charge of the WD, plus one dietician and a couple of nursing sisters. That didn't give them much leeway to choose friends. They were stuck with each other.

I remember an officer on our station asking a small group of us airwomen who shared a love for opera and symphonic music to come to her quarters one evening and play records. She served us coffee and cookies and we had a lovely time – particularly since it was somewhat illicit. But I'm convinced that what was done under excuse of "music appreciation" was more a case of her need for the company of kindred souls.

Our little bunch of music nuts was part of a larger clique known within and without as "the tribe." We took great pleasure in getting around the strict rules. One time we got into real trouble for some outrageous bit of rule-flouting, which was deemed to have undermined the discipline of the whole women's barracks. That same officer stamped into the barracks; confronted us and ripped a few shreds off us; then burst into tears, saying, "Dammit, you're making it so tough for me. Don't you realize that if I weren't an officer, I'd be a member of 'the tribe' too?" I remember feeling embarrassed, guilty, and terribly sad because I really liked her, and so did the others.

Former member, RCAF (WD)

She certainly had a soul

To my mind, there were some girls who didn't really want to become officers but they were forced into it, more or less, because somebody had to do it. There were certainly more headaches involved in being an officer and the pay wasn't that great either. And it was hard to adjust to having your friends in the ranks left behind.

A good officer, as far as I'm concerned, has to be human, like our CO She was much older than the rest of us, or so it seemed at the time. She was really kind to us; and she'd try to counsel us and keep us out of trouble as much as she could afford to, for the time she had. She took a personal interest in us as individuals . . . She certainly had a soul, that's for sure.

For some of them though, the rank went to their heads. I just wonder, if you could turn the clock back, with so many more women being educated today, what it would be like. I think it would be much different – an entirely different ball game – because men dominated the whole thing then.

Former member, CWAC

Some forms of activity could be made very interesting

One of the chief difficulties appears to be in organizing any form of activity for the off-duty hours for personnel living in barracks. I don't believe that this is as much of a problem in Training Centres as it is in the Companies where the personnel are employed in offices, etc. during the day and only come under the supervision of their own Company officers during the off-duty hours. It is appreciated that women cannot be regimented into organized sports but it is believed some forms of activity could be made very interesting, e.g., lessons in rifle shooting. The solution to this problem would appear to lie in better training of the officers in man management. Up to now, the Officers' Training Centre has been concerned chiefly with giving instruction in the fundamental military subjects which an officer must know and little time has been available for any training in man management.

D.N.D. H.Q. Memo re: CWAC personnel
June 8, 1943

We took off the cap and applied straws

One time we had a great party at the expense of a corporal whom most of us considered a pain in the neck. Somebody had seen her come back from leave and hide a bottle of rye among clothes in a zippered tote bag. Next time she was off the station, we decided to nip into her rye. Unfortunately the zipper was padlocked, and we weren't going to go in for any obvious vandalism. However, there was a gap of about an inch at the end of the zipper, so we took turns kneading the bag until we had worked the bottle

Private collection

Group of RCAF (WD)s.

into position so its neck came through the gap. Then we took off the cap and applied straws. The party got more hilarious as time went on, and eventually the bottle was empty. So, on went the cap, and the bottle was kneaded back into place. We watched the corporal for days, but she never cracked. After all, she couldn't report the loss. She wasn't supposed to have booze on the station at all!

Former member, RCAF (WD)

Experience will teach

It must be remembered that never before have women participated in any war to such an extent as they are today. Furthermore, officers of the CWAC are commissioned officers in every sense of the word. No doubt, in the beginning, male officers may find it strange to have the CWAC officers in their messes, but they should soon become accustomed to it and there is no reason why the customs and traditions of the Army should be placed in jeopardy . . . Even if soldiers were taught ferocity, it would certainly not intend to destroy in them all the amenities of social life . . . Should the policy prove at any time unworkable, it could be easily changed, but experience will teach. It should be given a real try-out.

Memo to Minister of Defence Ralston
From the Inspector General of Western Canada
June 6, 1942

National Archives of Canada, PA-128249

Members of CWAC Rifle Team practising on rifle range, Ottawa, Ont.,
March 1945.

They simply did not want women

The recruited officers (male) had the same outlook as if it were any other
job we all had to do together, but the permanent force officers were just
dreadful! They simply did not want women in the forces. They didn't
belong, and that was that. As for other women, they looked askance at
women in uniform. I don't know whether it was sour grapes or what, but,
there was definitely a feeling. For example, at the active service canteen,
women in uniform were not welcome in the least, with or without an
escort. That seemed ridiculous to me, but that was the way they wanted
to run it. They'd have girls come down in their little smocks to dance with
the men and they did have very good entertainment, but it was all
operated for the benefit of the men. Women in uniform just weren't
welcome on the premises.

At one point, I went to Lady Kemp who was honorary chairman of the
canteen, and told her I thought that their policy was absolutely iniquitous,
but I didn't get anywhere.

Overseas, of course, there was no problem. The ATS were asked into
the messes and canteens and no one gave it a second thought. Naturally
the people over here hadn't had the chance to see that side of the war, to

see what was going on there, or perhaps they would have had a different approach to the way they treated women in uniform.

Former officer, CWAC

You could tell who had money
You could tell who had money by their civilian clothes . . . But when we were all in uniform, everyone was the same.

Former member, RCAF (WD)

My mother had a charge account at Birks
My mother had a charge account at Birks, so the whole group of us waltzed in there one day and had the girl buff up the brass buttons on our uniforms – all at Mother's expense.

Former member, RCAF (WD)

What are friends for?
I guess a lot of the others resented us, because we had so much fun and we were generally in some kind of hot water, whereas they took the whole thing much more seriously – and there we were laughing and giggling our way through everything. It really seemed to burn them up when one of us was put "on charge" for something and had to wash windows or whatever, and the rest of us would pitch right in and help her – all strictly against the rules, of course – but what are friends for?

Former member, RCAF (WD)

I could see a civilian skirt underneath
They made a lot of stupid rules and people certainly did resent that aspect of being in uniform. Some women put in authority over other women turn out to be bullies and they take their own authority so seriously that they become totally inflexible. There was absolutely no bending of the rules for this type of officer.

For instance, there was a rule that you could not leave your quarters in civilian clothes, and so we would wear our uniforms out, go somewhere and change, and then return again wearing our uniforms at the end of the evening. After I became an officer, this didn't apply but my poor friends next door were still stuck with the rule. On one occasion, I found myself walking behind this girl who had on her regulation military raincoat and her military hat and was carrying an overnight bag. The problem was that she hadn't done up the button at the back of her raincoat, and I could see a civilian skirt underneath. So I stopped her and I could see her face sort of blanching and I said to her, "I thought you should know that you've left the back button of your raincoat undone." Very grateful, she quickly did it up and carried on her way. It was just that it seemed too ridiculous to pull rank in a case like that, even if I was being derelict in my duty.

Former officer, CWAC

Coffee, tea, milk, or pop

Many airwomen resented the fact that the men had their wet canteens where they could buy and drink beer, and women were stuck with tea, coffee, milk, and pop in theirs. Mind you, our crowd got around that sometimes by making a deal with the flight sergeant who ran the sergeants' mess. On special occasions, he'd hand beer out the back window to us under the cover of darkness and we'd smuggle it back to the women's barracks where we'd put it into the toilet tanks to keep cool. The system went undetected until the night all the labels floated off the bottles and plugged up the plumbing.

Former member, RCAF (WD)

That's the first thing I learned

I was shy with men . . . but I soon learned. They used to have these big dances when we were training at Rockcliffe, and if you stood all in a group together nobody would ask you to dance, but if just a couple of you stood a bit to one side, you'd be in business. That's the first thing I learned.

Former member, RCAF (WD)

The uniform didn't reform them

People behaved in uniform more or less as they behaved out of it. If they were poor types before they got in, the uniform certainly didn't reform them. There was a lot of talk about girls in uniform being prostitutes and so on, but what chance did a girl have to get much business if she was working all day and had to be in by ten or so every night? We did a lot of partying, there's no doubt of that, but not promiscuously. Not my group of friends, anyway.

Former member, CWAC

So young and so beautiful

Before this particular girl got discharged for pregnancy, I already knew there was something funny, because whenever she was ironing she always kept her coat on, even over her pyjamas. The poor thing was unmarried and she was terrified to go home to her parents, so her brother and sister said they'd take her in. Well, we got everything arranged for her, train tickets and so forth, and the station wagon was coming to pick her up at a friend's – to make sure she got away alright. The morning of the day she was due to leave, the sister called to say they'd thought it over and they had decided that they wouldn't take her after all. Then I had to go and find her where she was staying and tell her the news, and ask her if she wouldn't reconsider the idea of going home to her mother and father, because she had to go somewhere. So we called them. Then I had to put her on the train, knowing that her parents didn't really want her either. It was awful! She was so young and so beautiful, too.

Former member, WRCNS

You never knew for sure

From time to time somebody would be sent home. No explanation, they just disappeared. Pregnancy probably, but you never knew for sure.

Former member, RCAF (WD)

Because of her bulk

There was another woman, who was quite big naturally, who went up for a normal discharge. When she was checked out by the doctor, he discovered that she was eight months pregnant. Nobody had ever expected it because of her bulk. Discharge for pregnancy was called "Article 9" . . . She had thought she'd manage to get herself a regular discharge; in fact she'd already made all her own arrangements, on her own, to go the hospital in Halifax. She had found a room for herself and the baby, and then as soon as she could travel her parents were going to take them in, somewhere in a small town out West, and she was going to work in the family store and together they'd bring up the child.

Former member, WRCNS

National Archives of Canada, PA-128192

WRCNS personnel strike a pose in their dormitory, Halifax, N.S., May 1943.

A world of all women

It wasn't something I'd want to live through ever again . . . a world of all women. It brought out the best in a lot of people, but it also brought out the very worst in certain women, when they found themselves suddenly in positions of authority. A lot of pettiness cropped up when things got too top heavy.

Former officer, WRCNS

The major told her to lay off

I don't think anybody really gave much of a damn about it [homosexuality]. It was wartime and everybody had one thing in mind: win the war, and get the whole thing over with. There was no time for worrying about something that was considered basically unimportant at that time. As long as you were doing your job and doing it properly, nobody bothered much about the rest of it. Of course, if somebody was being obnoxious, that was another story. I remember one case where the one woman just wouldn't leave the other one alone and finally she got called in and the major told her to lay off, and that was the end of it. Believe it or not, most of the women in uniform were pretty decent. Sure there were a few who screwed around but on the whole, they certainly weren't doing anything more than a lot of women out of uniform when it gets right down to it. In fact, I think the civilians were worse.

Former member, CWAC

As if we were animals in a cage

We had an "Open House" on the station once and somebody overheard some of the visitors, two or three ladies, passing by an open window of the barracks. One said to the others, "That's where they sleep," sort of as if we were animals in a cage – as if we were some sort of strange beasts in a zoo. We all got a great laugh out of that.

Former member, RCAF (WD)

Roman Catholics, fall out!

On Sundays there was Divisions (which was a church service with everyone standing up), and it was mandatory. You lined up and marched to the service. Then the Roman Catholics would fall out for their service in the drill shed. If it was raining, a lot of people converted to the Catholic Church just for the occasion.

Former member, RCAF (WD)

My mother didn't believe it

Religious services were a priority. A priest was assigned to each camp. He heard confessions, said mass, gave out religious medals and holy pictures and prayer books – in English only. Mass might be celebrated at any hour. You had to adjust to this, but at least you were allowed to take communion even if you had already eaten, and on Fridays you could eat whatever you wanted to. The church had absolved us from meatless Fridays and our families as well if we were home on leave. My mother didn't believe it, though, so we never ate meat on Fridays, regardless of my special status.

In Moncton, the chapel was a great barracks. At one end was the section for the Roman Catholics, and at the other the part set aside for the Protestants. The same choir sang for both.

Former member, RCAF (WD)
(translation from French)

Canadian Forces Photographic Unit, DND, PL-17062

Invited guests of H.R.H. Princess Alice attend RCAF (WD) "At Home," Rockcliffe, Ont.

Only three bottles of beer, sir

After one of our nights on the town, we got paraded in front of this colonel on the base, and we all knew he was quite a drinker himself. They say he drank a bottle of rum and cream a day. Anyway, we got called in front of him and he asked me if I had anything to say for myself. Well, I said, "No, sir!" Then he asked me how much I'd had to drink and I told him only three bottles of beer (I didn't bother telling him they were quarts though). Then he said, "Well, you've got a pretty good record as a driver, so we'll let it pass with a warning this time. Just make sure it doesn't happen again." And, dammit, that very night the cook and his wife invited us out to a party, and when we were leaving he put a quart of beer in my battledress jacket, in the inside pocket. So we got back to the barracks and I forgot about this damn bottle, opened up my jacket for some reason and out fell the beer – smashed all over the place. Try and explain that one, when you've just gotten off one charge. So I said to myself, "You've really done it this time," and I had. Ten days confined to barracks. This time he didn't even ask for an explanation, and I lost ten days' pay too!

Former member, CWAC

I thought my hair was going to fall out

Everything was "dry" in Nova Scotia. You just couldn't get a drink unless you were in the men's mess or you had to sneak it. A fellow I knew in the Navy gave me some "pusser" rum once when I had a terrible cold. We were sitting in a restaurant and out came this coke bottle with rum in it. One sip, and I thought my hair was going to fall out. Talk about strong! It must have been 100 proof plus! And thick. It may not have done much for my cold, but it sure warmed me up in a hurry . . .

There was this one girl who used to come in regularly and tear up the barracks. They couldn't do a thing with her. She was built like a buffalo, too. Then somebody got the bright idea of putting her in the Provost Corps. They put her on the gate and anyone who came in drunk really got a going over from her. I don't think she ever took a drink from that time on.

Former member, WRCNS

Into the bushes

One night the station commander was walking along the playing field at the back and he fell over a couple who were having a little go at it. The airman leapt up, zipped himself up and saluted and said, "Good night, sir," and marched off. The WD ran off into the bushes. Naturally a great meeting of the WDs was called and this disgraceful conduct was revealed and the girl involved was requested to identify herself, otherwise we'd all be confined to barracks. Of course, nobody was going to confess. So, every night after supper, we'd be marched out to the parade square for about ten nights running, but nobody ever told who it was. We'd closed ranks on that one.

Former member, RCAF (WD)

Canadian Forces Photographic Unit, DND, PL-12097

RCAF (WD) Precision Squad smiling through the green curtains of their Pullman car as they embark on a three-week tour of the Prairie provinces and the Pacific Coast.

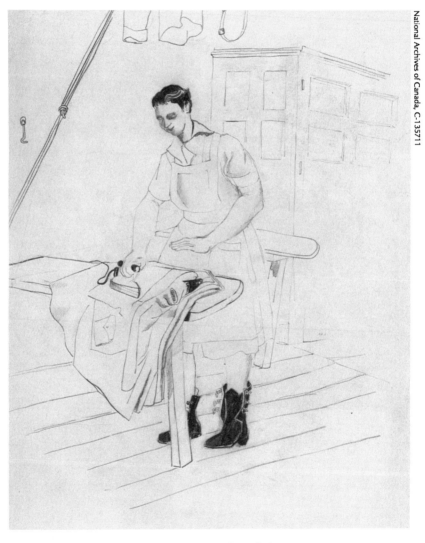

Molly Lamb Bobak, *CWAC Ironing*, December 1942.

FIVE

On Duty at Home and Overseas

ROM THE VIEWPOINT OF MOST women who "joined up," the most satisfying aspect of being in the service was their day-to-day work – satisfying in the sense that it gave a certain purpose to other less engaging elements of their existence. The regimentation, the rules and regulations that were meant to be followed to the letter, the lack of privacy, the fact that one's individuality seemed of little significance: all these were factors to be contended with, coped with, accepted if necessary (but not necessarily considered acceptable).

Once out of the barracks or off the parade square, however, the on-the-job duties contributed to a sense of purpose – and generally a more positive perspective. In the performance of their daily tasks, routine and monotonous though they may have been, there was nonetheless something about them that was more directly related to the war effort. To a degree, at least, they became a sort of reassurance that every service-woman was playing a small but vital part in the struggle against "the enemy." She could feel that, in effect, she was "doing her bit."

The ultimate aim for virtually every woman in uniform was, not unexpectedly, an overseas posting. The possibility that, in the process, there was a good chance that her life might be endangered (a number of the Canadian women serving overseas died during enemy air raids and other incidents while on duty) was rarely a deterrent. In fact, hardly anyone appears to have given it so much as a second thought. The desire to be as close to the action and to the boys overseas as possible, to have a real connection with what was happening, a first-hand experience, far outweighed any other considerations for most servicewomen, as it did for their male counterparts.

Statistically, aside from those women who served as nursing sisters, only about one in nine of the women who enlisted in Canada's armed forces was selected for overseas duty (from a total of over 45,000 servicewomen). Perhaps the danger factor was initially a deterrent in the eyes of those responsible for deployment of personnel. There is no doubt that once the air raids had abated to a degree, a larger number of women received postings overseas.

The initial suggestion that Canadian servicewomen might perform useful functions overseas came from Canadian Military Headquarters in London in February 1942. There was, it seems, a desperate need for laundresses. Civilian labour was virtually unavailable for such "less than vital" services. Would it not, therefore, be sensible to utilize Canadian servicewomen in this much-needed capacity? A detachment of 150 CWAC "other ranks" was duly requested.[1]

Members of the first RCAF (WD) contingent bound for overseas duty in England, spring, 1942.

Canadian Forces Photographic Unit, DND, PL-20327

Courtesy Thelma Thompson Murdoch

Three Manitoban airwomen, Shirley Stuart, Geraldine Reid, and Anne M. Hall, drafted for overseas duty in England.

The original qualifications for a CWAC servicewoman on overseas duty were three months of Basic Training. In addition there was an age limitation. She had to be over twenty-one and have a good medical record. (No doubt the inclemency of the British climate was being taken into account.) Further, she had to be "of exemplary character and possess a suitable temperament." "Appearance and general smartness" would also be a consideration in the choice of candidates for overseas duty. Just how much any of these stipulations had to do with performing the functions of a laundress is open to question but officially these were the requirements on record.[2]

There was one objection to the possibility of Canadian women serving in the United Kingdom. It would of necessity "create most difficult administrative problems." The usual bugaboo. It appears, however, that every rule must have its exception, and in view of the laundry dilemma at the Canadian base, expediency dictated concessions to the general rule of thumb. In this case, the laundry itself had not been constructed so there would be ample time to sort out the problems of accommodation and

National Archives of Canada, PA-129069

CWAC embarkation, Glebe Barracks, Ottawa, 1942.

supervision of personnel, which would in any event best be undertaken by the CWAC officers who accompanied the contingent.

The request for laundresses stated clearly that the release of these servicewomen was in the interest of manpower economy. As the senior official responsible put it, it was senseless "to tie up 150 men on the washing of clothes, when women could do the job just as well ... " Women, after all, were not needed on the front line and the situation had reached crucial proportions.

The approval from Canadian Military Headquarters in Ottawa reached London three months later. Yes, the laundresses would be dispatched and might it also be possible to employ Canadian servicewomen overseas in other capacities, should the necessity arise?

London responded almost instantly with a request for 200 clerks and suggested that since the laundry facilities were as yet incomplete, the request for clerical help might, in fact, take precedence. The total requirement (all ranks) was set at 400 and by late August 1942, London headquarters was in a position to accommodate over 500 CWAC personnel in three separate barracks.

Because of administrative delays, the promised accommodation was not ready for occupancy until two months later than originally planned; however, October 1942 saw the first draft of CWACs arriving in London. As it turned out, the arranged accommodation was a mansion of major proportions with only one minor drawback: in the interests of economy, only one telephone was placed at the disposal of the inhabitants for their personal use.

The October arrival of Canada's first "female soldiers" was heralded in the British press: "The Quacks have arrived in England to release fit men for more active service." Then just before Christmas, on December 19, 1942, a second group of 141 arrived. In March a third draft arrived and another in May of 1943. Finally, almost a whole year after the initial request, the laundresses landed, ready to do their bit.

According to plan, the CWAC personnel were to operate "under Army regulations – enforced, in so far as they can be made applicable . . . The Corps will be disciplined by its own officers and, in the event of adequate punishment being beyond the powers of the CWAC Officer, the offender may be tried by an Army Officer of Field Rank . . . The Army Act, with certain logical alterations, applies to the CWAC."[3]

In 1944, long-awaited permission came through for Canadian women who were already overseas to be enrolled as members of the CWAC. Two hundred and nineteen women were added to the roster with this new ruling, but of these, fifty-one had already been enlisted as members of the British counterpart, this having been their only option prior to the change in Canadian Army policy. By the war's end the number of Canadian women enlisted in Britain had risen to 313.

At about the same time, the possibility of sending women into the combat zones (behind the lines, of course) also came under consideration by Canadian Military Headquarters and by mid-April of 1944 this, too, was given the official nod. Women assigned to clerical duties could, no doubt, have been of great service; however, the first Canadian women to enter the "theatre of war" were four members of the CWAC performing with the Canadian Army Show in Italy. Subsequently, larger groups of CWAC officers and enlisted women (approximately 150) were dispatched to northwestern Europe, primarily to Belgium and Holland. And following the German surrender in May 1945, CWAC personnel were sent, both from Canada and from the United Kingdom, to take up administrative duties on the Continent.[4]

Photo by Alexander M. Stirton. National Archives of Canada, PA-139937

Officers observe graduation of first class of CWACs, London, England, February 19, 1943.

By the end of hostilities in the war zone on May 8, 1945, the CWAC (all ranks) numbered close to 2,000, and another 1,000 were allocated for overseas duty between May and October, 1945. In total, these 3,000 CWACs who served overseas comprised approximately 1.5 percent of the Canadian Army's population in the war zone.

The first RCAF (WD) contingent arrived in England in August 1942, just prior to the original CWAC company and close to a year after the formation of these two branches of Canada's armed forces. According to reports, the RCAF was hard pressed to keep up with the number of requests received from WDs hoping for an overseas posting. Over 1,300 eventually became part of the "lucky few."[5]

The Royal Canadian Navy originally made use of British Wrens in their overseas operations, but late in 1943 the first draft of Canadian WRCNS replacements arrived in the U.K. By the end of the war, the number of Canadian Wrens "on strength" in London, Plymouth, Greenock, and Londonderry was just over 500.[6]

There is, however, no question that the experience of overseas duty set these particular servicewomen apart from the rest. The "buzz bombs," the

First CWACs in Normandy, France (left to right: Ptes. Enid Powell, Murie Steward, Sgt. Linda Tuero, Vera Cartwright, all from Toronto, and Virginia Stanswell, Windsor, Ont.), Banville, France, July 30, 1944.

never-ending blackouts, the sound of sirens, the endless process of queuing up, became part of their day-to-day existence. As well, they were constantly exposed to the British bulldog spirit: the will to "muddle through" and maintain a sense of humour in the face of virtually any onslaught or adversity. These were, indeed, aspects of the war that were the unique experience of a relatively small number of Canadian servicewomen. They had been given the opportunity to live out the war under circumstances which were less removed from reality; and, almost without exception, they felt privileged and proud to be overseas and playing a part in the real war at closer range.

Notebook

Everybody wanted it!

Overseas duty? Everyone wanted it. I can't think of a single person who wouldn't have given her eye teeth to get over there. That was the whole point! And there was I, at Hagersville for the entire war . . . about twenty-

Canadian Forces Photographic Unit, DND, PL-22510

Newly arrived from Canada, a group of RCAF (WD)s overseas try on raingear and anti-gas equipment. (Left to right: Cpl. Barbara Bull of Oakville, Ont.; Leading Airwomen Rosalie Cutliffe of Brantford, Ont.; Mabel Gray of London, Ont.; Isobel White of Repley, Ont.; and Cpl. M. Wallace, Toronto.)

five miles from my home, except for a month's training in Ottawa and about six terrible days at Trenton. I certainly didn't see much of the war.

Former member, RCAF (WD)

The ultimate

Getting overseas was the ultimate for everyone – to get over closer to the action. Of course, we didn't know what it was really like. It was just the idea of the excitement and adventure of it all. We weren't even thinking of the dangers. Just like the men. They were the same. Getting overseas was what it was all about.

Former member, CWAC

You stayed dressed all the time

We were fourteen days getting across. Our route took us up by Iceland, and during the night sometimes the engines would all stop, so they could listen for signals, and if there were U-boats anywhere near, the destroyers

National Archives of Canada, PA-129093

Group of CWACs in lounge of ship en route to England, November 1942.

would go off and drop depth charges. You stayed dressed all the time, because it was so cold, and also you never knew when something might happen. There was lifeboat drill every morning.

Former member, RCAF (WD)

Lifeboats for three thousand
When we got word that the ATS needed more people and that some Canadian women might be called overseas, everybody was on cloud nine. When I went over it was on a sort of officer exchange scheme for three months. We were on the *Queen Mary* and she was never convoyed all the way because she was so fast. She could make it over in five or six days just zig-zagging across. When we got on board they told us that there were over 17,000 of us, but the lifeboat capacity was 3,000. For every meal there were three calls. Sometimes there was drill twice a day and you just lay in your berth with all your clothes on and your lifebelt beside you. But, being women, I suppose we at least had the security of knowing that we'd be given first choice for the lifeboats and so we had a better chance of surviving if anything happened.

We came well prepared for the journey, too. Instead of putting water in our waterbottles we filled them with Scotch. We sailed for about a day and a half unprotected, then for the next couple of days we had a convoy escort and when we approached Ireland, the Liberators flew out to keep an eye on us. We did sight a U-boat once, but they assured us that the *Queen Mary* could outrun a sub if she had to. Of course if one had managed to get close to us without being detected, we wouldn't have had a chance with all those men on board. The lifeboats wouldn't have been much use. But we still had to go through the drill anyway, twice a day, in the name of military protocol. We'd all be called up on deck just as if there might be an attack, and once the WD officer sent one of the girls back down below decks because she didn't have her pin on. There we were waiting to be torpedoed and she was down getting a tie pin!

Former member, RCAF (WD)

In a red-light house

Once we got to London we were split up; some of us to HQ, some of us to the Pay Office at Harrods and some to other places . . . perhaps to a particular squadron. And some of the places the girls found rooms in were pretty hilarious. A few of them even ended up in a red-light house their first night. But since we only had twenty-four hours to find a place to live before reporting back, you had to take what you could get.

I ended up climbing way up to the top floor of the place we'd found. After the voyage and carting all our stuff around all day trying to find a place we were all pretty bushed. Then during the night it started to rain, and the roof leaked and the water started just pouring in, and on top of it there was an air raid. Quite an introduction. The vibration knocked down a lintel from over the door of our room, so we soon learned to duck.

And it wasn't long till we were able to relocate to a really nice flat in a magnificent old Georgian house. The ceilings must have been eighteen feet high. The problem there was trying to keep the place heated during the cold weather. It got so bad that eventually we decided to find a smaller place with lower ceilings where we wouldn't freeze to death.

Former member, RCAF (WD)

Nobody told us a thing

It was freezing cold when we got to our station and the quarters weren't properly heated. If you wanted to be warm, you soon learned how to work

Unidentified RCAF (WD)s posing in their overseas "flat."

the fireplace. You were given a bag of coke every week and you had to get your own paper and your own kindling. We found out that if we got the downstairs fire going well enough, it would heat the water tank. Nobody told us a thing. We had to figure it out for ourselves. Just keeping warm was half the battle and we learned to scrounge pretty quickly.

Former member, RCAF (WD)

Four inches of water

There was a terrible shortage of water, only four inches of water for each bath, so we decided we could each take a bath every fourth day or else share the same bathwater. I always hated getting in last because there'd be all this scum on the top. It didn't take me long to develop the ability to take a scalding hot bath, so hot that none of the others could stand it, so I'd be first in.

Former member, RCAF (WD)

The real heroines

To my mind, the cooks were the real heroines. They got so little to work with and yet, somehow, they managed to make the meals reasonably appetizing for us. There was one egg per person per week, if that, and the rest of the time it was powdered eggs and sausages that tasted as though they were filled with sawdust with a little seasoning thrown in. But those cooks on overseas duty deserved a lot of credit. It was a pretty thankless job.

For those who could afford to splurge, fruit was almost always available at Harrods or Fortnum & Mason, but at an exorbitant cost. And people ate an awful lot of fish and chips, of course. Typical British fare even in wartime.

Former member, CWAC

Silk stockings won

My parents were British, but I was Canadian-born, so I could choose between the ATS and their dreadful stockings or the CWAC with their silk stockings. They won! And they had better pay, too.

Being in England, I was able to join up at eighteen. We did our Basic Training at Aldershot. All of us in the barracks together, and I felt like a baby compared to the girls sent over from Canada who had to be twenty-one. But that's how I got my education – from all those older CWACs. They even got a book for me at one point. I thought I knew enough to stay out of trouble, but I guess they decided there was more I should know. And of course I wasn't going to give them the satisfaction of reading it in front of them, but the minute they were out the door naturally I had my nose right into it.

Former member, CWAC

Eight till eight

We would go on parade, and then we'd start to work at eight in the morning, and often not get out of there until eight at night, and we rarely got any leave. They couldn't keep up with the volume of work at HQ until towards the end of the war, when there were more WDs sent over.

Former member, RCAF (WD)

A Canadian woman's voice

The Army gradually became more conscious of the need for good public relations, and so the Canadian officer in charge of broadcasting asked me it I'd do a few bits and pieces for a broadcast he was sending back to Canada depicting life overseas. He needed a Canadian woman's voice.

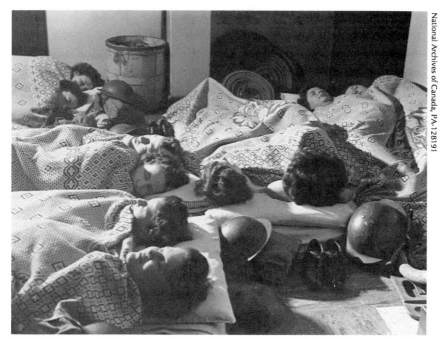

National Archives of Canada, PA-128191

WRCNS personnel sleeping in quarters at Canadian Naval Mission Overseas, London, England, July 25, 1944.

Then, after D-Day, I was taken on by the BBC to work for them in broadcasting, and it was enormously exciting. The program was called "The Allied Expeditionary Forces Program," and was directed towards Americans, Canadians, and British troops.

The hours were peculiar, given the nature of the job, but it was so interesting that you really didn't mind how many hours you worked; in fact, the more the better. We'd be on for six hours, starting in the morning, and then rotate so that the second day, you'd be on during the middle of the day, and then broadcasting at night the third day. Then, we'd be off three days, unless something came up. If we were doing the early BBC broadcast, we'd sleep overnight in the concert hall. It was on a lower level (underground), and we'd take a mattress on the steps of the concert hall for the night and then get up at five to be on the air by six.

Former member, CWAC

I could barter my cigarettes
Mail got pretty high priority. It helped keep up everyone's spirits. And the parcels would come in batches – not with any regularity. You never knew

when the next batch would arrive. I'd get about 300 cigarettes every month, and because I didn't smoke, I could barter them . . .

As for letters home, you'd rarely have time to sit down and write a whole letter at one sitting, and so you'd write a little each day; and then after a week had gone by, you'd stick it in the mail. Then, after that, it would be opened to make sure there was no vital information being leaked out.

Former RCAF (WD)

You'd hear this buzzing noise

At one stage, the bombing was so bad that they thought they might have to evacuate Headquarters. The V-1's were really awful. You'd hear this buzzing noise – it was the engine inside the rocket – and when it stopped, you knew the bomb was about to drop. They sent them over without a break for three or four days running, and our own guns never stopped. There was this constant bombardment. You couldn't sleep because of the din and you never knew when one was going to land on top of you. That was probably the worst bombing I can remember.

A lot of people slept in the "Tubes," and we'd see these little tykes going off to school in the mornings with their faces black from the soot down in the Tube stations.

Former member, RCAF (WD)

Little crosses in the sky

The doodle-bugs (buzz bombs) used to come over in great numbers, and the RAF would send up planes to nudge them around so they'd be aiming back in the direction they'd come from. This was a pretty risky business. From the higher floors of the BBC where I worked, you could actually see them coming towards London: little crosses in the sky with fire spouting from the rear, making this "putt-putt-putt" sound, and when the sound cut out, you knew it was out of fuel and about to drop. Then there'd be the noise of an explosion, and you knew you were one of the lucky ones.

Former member, CWAC

Twenty to an ambulance

During the raids, we were driving staff cars, Daimlers and Rolls Royces and so forth. Then when we'd get back we'd have to take the ambulances out to the areas that had been hit, and take the injured people to hospitals

#42 Company CWAC party for war orphans, England, December 1943.

or first aid clearing stations, sometimes twenty to an ambulance, crammed in every which way.

The amazing thing to me – to all of us – was that none of these people took their injuries very seriously. They'd want to get right back to work with bandaged arms or legs or heads.

Army HQ Staff Driver (Special Division)

My knees were shaking

During one raid in the little Blitz of 1944 in London, I discovered afterwards that my knees were shaking. I hadn't really been aware of how scared I was, until then. It was entirely an involuntary action on the part of my knees.

At another point, I was being interviewed by a Canadian war correspondent, and we agreed to meet for lunch at a pleasant little place I knew of. As it happened, there was a nice table at the window, but at her suggestion we took a table towards the back. Sure enough, one of the V-1's landed about a block away. It blew the front window right out of the restaurant. This little waitress standing close by threw her apron over her head and her shoulders started heaving. When I went over to comfort her, she said, "I'm not frightened, but I think I'm going to throw up!" . . . and away she went.

Former officer, CWAC

Sweeping up glass

Sweeping up glass, that's one of the most horrible sounds in the world. In the mornings we'd see the people out there sweeping up the glass from all the windows that had blown out during the last raid. And there was no glass available to replace it, so people just made do with cardboard, or newspaper – whatever they could get to try to keep the cold out.

Former member, RCAF (WD)

Quite a fright

Driving to the clearing stations or hospitals during a raid was pretty hair-raising, except at the time you didn't really stop to think about it, you just did what you had to do. Sometimes you'd be driving somewhere and suddenly there'd be a pile of rubble in front of you, and you'd have to back up and try another route . . .

In '44 everybody was wanting a child, because you never knew whether or not your husband would make it back. I was pregnant and drove right up to the last month. Then I went into the hospital at Bramshot, south of London. When Wayne was only a few days old (he was the only baby in the nursery), he disappeared. Vanished into thin air during a raid. After the raid, when they discovered he was missing, they had an all-out search because they were convinced that he must be somewhere within the hospital, but where? With wounded being brought in continually, it took them about twenty-four hours to track him down, in one of the Canadian officers' rooms. He'd seen him in the nursery earlier, and, during the raid, he just got this crazy idea that he wanted to take the baby and hold on to it for a while. Then when the baby started to cry, he went to the dining room, ate his meal, and came back with milk and orange juice and fed Wayne with a spoon, and decided, I guess, that things were going pretty well, so why not keep him a little longer? Until eventually they discovered what had been going on, and brought him back to the nursery. It was quite a fright! Then within two or three weeks, I was back driving again . . .

Former Army HQ driver (Special Division)

A disembodied trance

Boys coming back from the front on leave knew they'd have to go back and some of them looked in pretty bad shape. They'd have this glassy look in their eyes and they wouldn't talk much, if at all. They seemed almost in a kind of a trance . . . a disembodied trance. One fellow I knew actually predicted that this would be his last leave. I can still hear him saying it and sure enough, he went back and his jeep drove over a land mine just a few days later.

Former member, CWAC

A horrible sight

We were sent to an air station where we were the only Canadian girls and when we first got there, they wouldn't tell us what the code-names for the targets meant – "Fish" or "Trout" or "Whitebait." We were only women and sergeants, but after a while that attitude changed. There was even a code-name for the strips of aluminium that they used to drop over enemy territory to confuse their radar. It was called "Window" – narrow strips of heavy foil in various widths.

The bombers took different routes, depending on the weather. One time in '44 a bad storm came in from Norway and created bad icing conditions. Out of the six squadrons on our base, we lost seven planes that night. Some crashed before they ever got out of England because of ice on the wings. It was a horrible sight. We actually watched some of them come down, with seven men in each plane. And others were still taking off while their pals were coming down.

Maybe this sounds hard-hearted, but we used to have a pool – sort of like a hockey pool – to see who would get back from "ops" [operations] first. And the pilots all knew we had a shilling on who'd be first in, so they'd try to cut their routes here and there. Some of them never did get back, and as time went on some of them got very superstitious. One chap I knew had to take up a different plane from the one he normally flew and after they'd gone so far they radioed that they were turning back because of some sort of mechanical failure. Actually there wasn't a thing wrong with the aircraft. It was just that none of them felt secure, so they decided to head back to the base.

Every time the planes came back from ops they'd put up three searchlights called Sander lights and then gradually they'd start calling them down . . . One day I was out watching take-offs when one of the "kites," as they called them, suddenly veered off the runway onto the grass. Eventually it came around and tried a second take-off. Same thing, only this time the undercarriage collapsed and the whole crew evacuated. By this time I was back in the control tower because they were afraid she might go up. And sure enough. There was this orange flash of light and she was gone.

When Mackenzie King came to visit the base, they wanted to put on a big show to impress him. Unfortunately the weather was dreadful and normally they would have scrapped the whole thing. But they were determined to go on with it, until some of the boys refused to go up. I guess they didn't think that Mackenzie King was worth risking their lives for. Basically nobody was very impressed by him, anyway.

Former member, RCAF (WD)

Pte. Barbara Cummings and Pte. Jean Gallant, CWAC entertainers in the Army Show, Netherlands, February 28, 1945.

Photo by Ken Bell. National Archives of Canada, PA-139940

A couple of German soldiers

I went straight into the Army Show from Basic Training. They knew I had experience in entertainment and when they came to Kitchener and announced that they would be holding two days of auditions, I signed up right away. An unbelievable number of people turned out and I was one of the lucky two they selected to go to Toronto to start rehearsing. We stayed in a rooming-house near the rehearsal hall.

We'd be at the hall all day long, standing around for hours. There was a line-up of dancers and soloists and group singers and then little skits in between. Altogether there were about thirty of us in the show and none of us had known each other before we were all thrown in together. But doing that kind of work it doesn't take long for everyone to feel part of the group, and we were all more or less the same age. Of course, we also knew right away that we'd be heading overseas, so the excitement really built up as we were rehearsing.

When we did get over there we performed in England, and then in Holland and Belgium. Once Germany surrendered we performed there too, but we did the majority of our shows in Holland. In some of the cities there seemed to be virtually no civilians. It was just the Army and ourselves. You'd see houses with gardens in full bloom and the doors standing open, but no people. And because the Germans had left explosives behind, every inch had to be checked out first, so we couldn't get out and wander around on our own.

I remember picking dozens and dozens of flowers from the gardens, because there was nobody there to enjoy them. I made corsages, and we wore them in our hair and put bouquets in our rooms. Then if we performed for civilians in places where they'd been allowed back, we'd be given so many flowers afterwards that we ended up giving them to the hospitals as well.

Somewhere in Holland, we were going along in convoy when one of the trucks broke down. While we were sitting there waiting, some of the fellows started playing just to pass the time, and pretty soon a crowd gathered, and then we girls started our dance routine. Before we knew it everyone was out there dancing in the street.

Usually we had no idea where we'd be performing. It could be in a theatre or an auditorium or on a makeshift stage at someone's estate. And sometimes, if there weren't too many Army personnel in a particular area, we'd invite the locals to the show. Naturally they just loved it, after all they'd been through.

In one town we played in, one of our girls had a nasty scare. She'd wandered up to the third floor of this old theatre we'd been rehearsing in – just killing time and looking around between numbers – when all of a sudden she looked up for some reason. There was a trap door in the ceiling and there were these two male faces peering down at her. She nearly had a fit and came running back to report that she'd seen these two fellows in the attic. At first no one really took her seriously but sure enough, it turned out that they were a couple of German soldiers who'd either deserted or been left behind, so they were taken prisoner right on the spot.

Former member, CWAC Army Show

Members of the first contingent of CWAC personnel to enter Germany, June 12, 1945. (Left to right: Sgt. Jane Shaddoch, Pte. Polly Pollyblank; Pte. Martin Macpherson at rear.)

Photo by Karen M. Hermiston. National Archives of Canada, PA-128229

It really did something to me
The first time I went over to the Continent, the Germans were still bombarding the coast of France, and we had to dodge the flak. We put down in Brussels and I was billeted in a hotel there. From there we went north by car. The destruction everywhere was just incredible. We drove between piles of rubble as high as a house. Whole towns were obliterated. You'd see the people out in the fields with Sterno cans trying to cook and a pathetic piece of canvas over them as shelter of sorts.

Never will I forget that drive! You could see people sort of prodding through the ruins and then just standing . . . looking. I saw one man and a small boy getting bricks out by hand and trying to build a little house in a clearing. Here and there graves of Canadian soldiers with daffodils placed on them lovingly . . . and everywhere the forests were seared and scorched and burned, with new green coming up and yards and yards of white tape around trees marking land mines. An unforgettable sight!

On a subsequent trip I stayed with the Vaniers in their flat in Paris. it was spacious beyond belief and they were both incredibly kind and gracious. It was marvellous to see the effects of the pinpoint bombing all around the city. Somehow they'd managed to miss all the beautiful buildings and just hit the strategic targets – railway stations and so forth. Everywhere the French were talking about the amazing accuracy of the RAF bombing. And the Canadians were also considered tops. We could get anything and could do no wrong, whereas the Americans, for whatever reason, had failed to endear themselves. Perhaps they gave the impression that Paris belonged exclusively to them. Who knows?

During my stay in Paris I did the rounds of the servicewomen's hostels and clubs, then I headed back to Brussels, where I toured more service clubs and interviewed some of our CWAC girls. A number of them were working out of Ghent on the Army card index of casualties. They were working shifts so I couldn't manage to get them all together; however, I spoke to as many of them as I could individually. It seemed to give them a lift.

Former commanding officer, CWAC

Canadian Forces Photographic Unit, DND, PL-26758

Leading Airwoman Ethel Thompson of Marshall, Sask., hangs out the washing. In background are Nissen huts which served as overseas accommodation for some airwomen posted for duty in northern England.

Eeee, what a posh job!

The underground factories in Britain were astounding: blocks and blocks with streets and avenues just like a little underground town or industrial area. There were mainly munitions and aircraft factories that had to be protected from enemy bombing. They were very hush-hush, of course, and everything was under way around the clock. They literally never stopped production.

We military types weren't very popular with the Englishwomen working in the factories. When we drove official visitors through in these big limousines, they would yell out things like, "Eeee, what a posh job!" What they never realized was that we also drove ambulances and trucks carrying explosives and that it wasn't at all as posh as it appeared to be.

Former Army HQ driver (Special Division)

Woe is me!

There was a poem that I saved because it said a lot about the predicament we were in overseas, with all the secrecy and security measures. All those slogans like "loose lips sink ships" . . .

Woe is me
You asked me to write
Now what will it be?
I can't write a thing
'Cause it's censored, you see.

Can't mention the weather
Whether raining or shine.
'Bout all I can say is
That I'm feeling fine.

Can't say that we're drafted.
Can't say where we'll go
One reason for that is
We usually don't know.

Can't mention the work
That we're doing each day
And it's hardly worth mentioning
The wages they pay.

Can't take any snaps
Within miles of shore
There's really not much
We can do any more.

Can't keep a diary
About what we do.
Just hello and goodbye
If I telephone you.

If we tell any secrets
We're sure in a spot.
We're C.B.d for two weeks
If perchance we get caught.

Please write and remember
In spite of the wars
Write all that you know
'Cause they don't censor yours!

Former member, WRCNS

Canadian Forces Photographic Unit, DND, PL-23683

RCAF (WD)s arrive for duty on Pacific Coast, 1944.

The entire complement of Canadian servicewomen on overseas duty, in all three services, was only slightly over 5,000, but in the eyes of friends who stayed behind they were the chosen few, on whom Fortune had truly smiled. Although the degree of glamour attributed to overseas service was considerably removed from reality, it seemed an enviable lot to the women left behind. Anything, it seemed to them, would be preferable to sitting in the middle of the Prairies or on an isolated Newfoundland air station, or watching and listening for enemy aircraft hour after hour in a tiny observation hut on Vancouver Island's west coast. While the performance of such duties was clearly vital to the war effort, it offered absolutely no adventure or romance. It is hardly surprising, then, that many servicewomen left on Canadian soil felt a certain sense of frustration and disappointment at having been passed over by the luck of the draw. The real war was happening somewhere else.

Those women assigned for duty on Canada's east coast, especially in the Halifax area, probably came closer to the reality of the war being waged overseas than any other servicewomen on this side of the Atlantic. In Newfoundland's air stations, WDs were able to pick up signals on their headsets from the flights *heading overseas, literally hundreds of aircraft on their way across to help increase Allied air power.*

In Halifax and environs, WRCNS plotters vigilantly kept track of all shipping in the Gulf and the North Atlantic, including the whereabouts of German U-boats. From time to time, a U-boat would manage to slip through the net and make its silent passage up the St. Lawrence River. Occasionally, it would find a target, and when this happened, the plotters were among the first to know.

Notebook

We could sleep at all hours, or on a table-top

In our plot room in Halifax, we kept track of all shipping on the North Atlantic. Gales, broken ships, U-boats, and changes of course were part of our daily life. The war seemed very close. We shared operations headquarters with the Air Force. When possible, they gave air coverage, but on this side of the Atlantic, it was mostly a naval job.

Photo by Subt. H.H. Black, National Archives of Canada, PA-107099

WRCNS personnel operating switchboard, HMCS Stadacona, Halifax, N.S., March 3, 1943.

From Stadacona, all the Wrens that worked at operations headquarters were taken to work by bus. Since we were all watchkeepers, we had irregular hours. This had its compensations too, so nobody seemed to mind too much. We were young and could sleep at all hours, or on a tabletop. These girls were a great group – signal women, coders, plotters, etc. We were all doing important work and found it interesting. In the WRCNS, as in every service, there were all kinds: the good, the bad, and the indifferent. Life was what you made it, but not everybody could fit in.

In June 1944, with two other plotters, I was drafted to HMCS *Bytown* in Ottawa, to take a plotters' course at operations headquarters. At the end of this course, we were confirmed as "leading Wrens," and I returned to Halifax to another winter of storms and losses; as well as the steady line of supplies reaching England. There were U-boats on the Atlantic coast; one night our bus was late because they had been using it to take survivors to the hospital.

Former member, WRCNS

Massive flights

The problem was that Newfoundland weather – being what it is! You could sit there with the headsets on for a whole shift and hear absolutely nothing, sometimes even for days and days at a time. And then, suddenly, there'd be these massive flights, hundreds of aircraft, coming in from Bangor, Maine. We'd pick them up on our sets as they were on their way over, headed across the Atlantic.

Former member, RCAF (WD)

Action on board

Most Canadians had no idea just how close those German U-boats got – way up the St. Lawrence. And sometimes the girls who were plotters in Halifax would stay up half the night, after their shifts, because of all the action on the board. They said they just had to stay and see what developed. Those plotters had to be good, too. Most of them were extremely bright – they had to be – and devoted to their jobs. They often worked hours overtime, and contributed a great deal.

Former member, WRCNS

You can take your mask off, now

Getting overseas wasn't that easy. You really had to know somebody, or be essential in some capacity over there. Every Wednesday in Halifax, we'd have to put on our gas masks and then get right back to work. We'd keep them on for a while and then the signal would come that we could remove them. Of course, it was standard practice to come up to someone who was still working away with their mask on, lean over and say, "You can take off your mask, now!" Lord, they were ugly things! There was one place at the side where you could listen on the phone, but the whole outfit was so terrible to get into, and you had to remember to blow out instead of in . . . Evidently only the Wrens in Halifax went through this drill regularly, because we were close to the action . . .

Towards the end of the war, you'd be at church and the minister would announce during the sermon that there were ships being sunk right outside Halifax harbour. You'd hear the sirens and the ambulance.

Former member, WRCNS

It would have been curtains
About the second day after I'd arrived on station in Hagersville, Ontario, I got the grand tour and right in the midst of it the alarm bells started going off like crazy. People were running around madly and it was general pandemonium. Looking out the control tower window, we could see a plane coming in very low. The pilot appeared to have nicked the tower with the tip of his wing, then his other wing struck the telephone pole at the side of the hangar next to us, which spun him right round and he walked away. Of course, if he'd ever hit the tower it would have been curtains for all of us. It was certainly an exciting introduction to the Air Force. I guess it's surprising that more of those pilots weren't killed during their training, because they were all very young and very green, but when it did happen, it cast an awful pall over the whole station.

Former member, RCAF (WD)

Night rides
I spent three years in Kingston, Ontario. We used to laugh and say it was like being in the penitentiary there. We were actually at Fort Frontenac most of the time and at that point they were sending out a lot of night convoys on training exercises so we got to know quite a number of the fellows involved, and since we were always short of money (from going out and living it up) we used to take the gas cans that were stored on the sides of the trucks while we were out on these night rides. We had it

Department of National Defence

Member of WRCNS preparing to raise ship's flag, Halifax, N.S.

cooked up so that whenever we stopped we'd drop off one of the cans of gas and stash it. Then the next day we'd go back, pick it up, and sell it for extra money.

Later I was assigned to drive a ration truck – hundreds of pounds of butter in one truckload. We'd transport the stuff from one mess hall to another and we'd do a little business on the side because we knew a lot of civilians who'd be happy to have it at almost any price. Usually they'd arrange to meet us at different places along the route where we could stop the truck and give them their little bundles of butter.

Former member, CWAC

Sitting ducks
You were completely alone up there in the control room when you were on night duty, from midnight until 5:30 a.m., and it was very lonely work. Once an hour you'd have to go down this darkened corridor, then down a flight of stairs and outside, to read the darn Stephenson screen for the wind speed and so forth. There didn't seem to be a human being for miles

and sometimes I got a creepy feeling sitting up there all alone. You couldn't hear anyone approaching because the teletype machine was going all the time. Not that anything ever actually happened but it really started to bother me and I found that I was listening for imaginary noises all night long. Thinking back on it, I realize that it obviously hadn't occurred to anyone that WDs on night duty were so isolated and exposed. If anyone had wanted to jump us, we'd have been sitting ducks up there all alone. No wonder I was close to panic sometimes.

And it wasn't just humans you had to worry about. One night when I came on duty right there at the foot of the stairs there was this enormous rat that had been caught in a trap. But boy, he sure wasn't dead . . . just mad! Well, I decided right then and there that this was something I could not handle on my own, so I called one of the firemen to come over and do something about it. When he finally turned up, I think he was even more scared than I was, but he did manage to bash him with his fire axe and that was that.

Former member, RCAF (WD)

"Jesus Loves Me"
When I used to have to go out on "local purchases" to Simcoe or Brantford, I'd always try to get this one particular driver because she could sing "Jesus Loves Me" in Chinese. Her parents had been missionaries in China. The minute we'd get into town we'd head straight for the Chinese cafe and she'd start singing in return for coffee and doughnuts on the house. For them it was a great joke and they always made us feel very welcome.

Another of my finest hours was when the stationary engineer came to me with a requisition order for a "worm," something to do with a boiler, I gather. So I called up this place in Galt – Babcock, Wilcox, Goldie & Mc-Cullough – and after I'd given the fellow on the order desk the number of this thing . . . this "worm," he asked me how I wanted it sent. "Oh, just put it in an envelope and mail it," I told him. There was a sort of dead silence on the other end of the phone and then in a quiet voice he inquired whether I had ever seen a "worm." I admitted that indeed I had not but that he should just send it along whichever way he thought best.

So about three or four days later, while I was at the usual Friday night service dance, I received a call from the gatehouse that they needed me to take a delivery. There I was having a fine time, whooping it up, so I said, "Oh, just leave it there and I'll sign for it tomorrow." Nothing doing! And when I got myself to the gate I understood why: my "worm" turned out to be about sixteen feet long and was sitting on a sort of flatbed truck.

Being assigned to local purchases also involved a weekly visit to Parke, Davis – the big wholesale drug outfit. There was this old chap I usually dealt with without any problems, but one day he wasn't there for some reason, so I gave my purchase voucher to this young fellow. It was for twelve gross of condoms. I guess I'd led a pretty sheltered life because I'd never even heard of the word let alone its purpose in life, so I had no idea what I was ordering.

Well, this guy looked at the order and then he looked at me. "Do you think that's gonna be enough?" he asked with a sort of a leer on his face. And in my innocent state I asked him if he thought I should double the order. Then with an even bigger leer he asked me what I had in mind. Just then the old boy appeared on the scene. I guess he'd heard the conversation. Anyway he asked to see my purchase order and then told me I shouldn't be responsible for this order and to go and get my driver to handle the situation. I was still none the wiser till I got back to the station with the voucher and handed it to my sergeant, who then quietly took me back into the dispensary and passed on to me one more of the facts of life.

Former member, RCAF (WD)

Someone had to do it
My job was to list all the equipment issued to airmen. It was tedious work because it was always exactly the same list, but someone had to do it . . . Then when I'd read the casualty lists in the papers, I'd say to myself, "It's true, I am doing something to help, but the boy I've relieved for overseas duty might very well end up getting himself killed." So my sentiments were mixed. It was hard to know what was right.

Former member, RCAF (WD)
(translation from French)

RCAF (WD)s Dorothy Case, Eileen Belanger, Lucette Laporte, and Edith Lowe at #13 Service Flight Training School, St. Hubert, Que., assisting in handling stores for barracks, March 21, 1942.

Molly Lamb Bobak, *Train's Dining Car*, February 1943.

SIX

Off Duty

F OR SERVICEMEN AND SERVICEWOMEN alike, "off-duty" time was a precious commodity. Even if it only consisted of a brief forty-eight-hour pass, at least for a few hours they could let off steam and try to forget about anything but making the most of every precious minute. All too soon, the term of respite would be over.

As one former servicewoman described the situation: "We worked very hard, so when it was time to play, we played hard, too. Unfortunately, our 'play time' was very limited. Aside from evenings out, there were a prescribed number of forty-eight- and seventy-two-hour passes – depending on rank and so forth – and then everyone was entitled to their two weeks off per year. It didn't seem like much."

Even for noncombatants, the desire to relax was scarcely unnatural. The salutary effect of getting away from the wearisome daily regimen, even for a day or two, helped to make being back on the job slightly less tedious and confining. Even something as simple as being able to eat whatever and whenever one wanted to was a welcome change. The opportunity to become an unprogrammed individual – a free spirit – was something everyone in uniform looked forward to, regardless of rank or position.

Many women in the services, whether stationed within Canada or on overseas duty, took advantage of their leaves to see something of the surrounding countryside, cycling, walking, taking picnics, and generally exploring. To a degree this also helped make it easier to get through the on-duty hours with at least a few pleasant memories to think back on.

Photo by Capt. F.L. Dubervill. National Archives of Canada, PA-116744

St. Valentine's Day dance held by CWAC personnel at Canadian General Headquarters, Brussels, Belgium, February 14, 1944.

For those stationed overseas the possibility of getting home was clearly not an option and in any case, for most servicewomen overseas, time off was at a premium. The quest for distant relatives was a major preoccupation for many of those given postings in the U.K., and once long-lost or distant family members had been located, visits usually ensued. For other servicewomen, discovering rural Britain became an adventure in itself. Occasionally solo, but more often in pairs or a group, they would strike off for a brief respite from the ever-present reality of the war – to stroll or cycle along country roads or visit local historic sites.

In any event, from the standpoint of those in charge, the paramount concern appears to have been the maintenance of a good public image for service personnel in uniform while on a pass or on leave. The dubious reputation of servicewomen, especially on the home front, had become a worrisome matter. For one thing, a negative public perception of women in uniform could affect recruitment, and, in any case, the honour and reputation of the respective services should be upheld.

The advent of women in the military was already an unprecedented break with tradition and the notion that servicewomen might be regarded as camp followers in disguise must be proven false at all costs. For the authorities, the only possible way to accomplish this was to ensure that off-duty appearance and conduct were exemplary at all times. In practice, this was not always the case – there were sufficient incidents on record in all three of the women's services to warrant concern. Despite the fact that an equal, if not greater, number of civilian women might be accused of immoral behaviour and promiscuity, servicewomen in uniform were highly visible and hence more open to criticism.

In all three services a great deal of consideration appears to have been given to the forewarned-is-forearmed theory. Every attempt was made to ensure that each and every woman in uniform was aware that excessive familiarity with the opposite sex (in or out of uniform) could breed more than contempt. Lectures, films, and directives addressing the incipient problems brought on by "fraternization" were widely circulated as a means of protecting innocent and ignorant alike. However well intended they may have been, these efforts were more often a source of amusement than any sort of effective vehicle for education or prevention.

Regulations regarding deportment and general appearance while in uniform were clearly defined. To the chagrin of the authorities, however, these regulations were often interpreted somewhat differently by servicewomen liberated from their station or barracks. Reports of flagrant violations were a persistent aggravation to commanding officers. The rules and regulations pertaining to off-duty dress and deportment were intended to be both clear and reasonable, but many of those to whom these directives applied chose to interpret them differently or ignore them altogether.

Notebook

The Army owned you
The one thing that we all had in common was the feeling that you were limited, that the Army owned you, in a way. We couldn't just come and go as we pleased. You had to have a pass and you had to ask for it.

Former member, CWAC

Canadian Forces Photographic Unit, DND, PL-36712

After the game, RCAF personnel return to the base.

Getting around the rules

Plotting occupied a lot of our time. We'd have our meetings – generally in the shower room at night and mostly it was concerned *not* with getting off the base, but with getting back on again if you knew you were going to be out past the ten-thirty curfew time. One night we were trying to sneak back onto the base and we thought that if we cut across the runway carrying branches in front of us, they'd think we were trees. We didn't get away with that one. They swung the searchlight beam around and there we were, lit up like Christmas trees standing with our branches on the tarmac ... I was always "on charge" for something or another. You certainly couldn't say that I was a model airwoman.

> Former member, RCAF (WD)

Leaving with all the dirty laundry

This friend and I both had dates and we were supposed to "clean ship" because it was Tuesday night. Well, we had to figure out how we could get off. My friend was a sick-berth attendant and she was the one who came up with an idea. She knew that at such and such a time a truck would be leaving with all the dirty laundry, so we somehow got ourselves into the back of the truck and away we went. Getting back wasn't such a problem because they'd automatically assume that we had a pass.

Former member, WRCNS

Jammed with sailors
Our curfew was very early in Halifax. We didn't have nearly the freedom that some people on other bases had. For one thing, Halifax was usually jammed with sailors from all over the place – merchant ship crews as well . . . Ten o'clock was our curfew, with one midnight pass a week, which you had to have if you wanted to go to a show, because you'd have to line up for at least two hours before you could even get in, let alone watch the movie. It was the same in restaurants. You lined up even to get something to eat. By the end, everybody was fed up, civilians and service people alike, always having to line up no matter where you went or what you did. The city was just plain overcrowded, and it made for a lot of tension.

Former member, WRCNS

A female Captain Bligh
On one leave my forty-eight-hour uniform nearly did me in. My uncle had invited me to a party and there I was sporting a set of RAF buttons a chap I knew had given me (because they shone far better than ours did) plus a round-collared shirt, a knitted tie, and nylon stockings to boot – all I needed was high heels! All of a sudden I looked around and, to my horror, there was a British WAAF officer (very high-ranking, too) standing with her hands clutched behind her looking very much like a female Captain Bligh. Naturally she was wearing no makeup and her hair was tightly done up, while mine was nice and loose and trailing over my collar.

It turned out that she had been one of the British advisors sent out to consult about the formation of the WDs and she kept asking me all sorts of questions about life on the station. I laid it on thick, of course, about how good the food was and how pleasant the quarters were and so on. I didn't have enough arms and legs to cover all my anti-regulation sins and still she went on questioning me, as I went on "Yes, Ma'aming" all over the place. Finally she went on her way, telling me what a credit I was to the service. My God, if she'd only known!

Former member, RCAF (WD)

On would go the nylons

Whenever we went on leave, the first thing we'd do was take off that terrible new-issue cap that sort of stood straight up and replace it with the old one that we far preferred. Next would be the lisle stockings. Off they'd go and on would go the nylons and perhaps a good "officer-type" men's shirt that you'd saved up for and bought in Toronto for such occasions at great expense.

Former member, RCAF (WD)

All the booze we wanted

The hotel was the only place where you could go to have a drink. Saturdays were always wild and there'd be fights among the civilians and while they were going at it, we'd be busy swiping all the beer off the tables. So our table was always loaded with beer we hadn't paid for . . . We just lived each day as it came along. If somebody said, "There's a party tonight," then we'd be off. A couple of times another friend and I were confined to barracks for being late for parade. Somehow we managed to get ourselves over to the kitchen of the officers' mess because we knew all the cooks from delivering rations. We'd have all the booze we wanted down there and then we'd sort of stagger back to our bunks.

Former member, CWAC

Going out in uniform

When I was stationed at Rockcliffe, going out in uniform created a few problems for me because my beau was a squadron leader. He couldn't take me out anywhere for dinner since officers were not permitted to socialize publicly with women in the ranks . . . Of course we found a way around it. Everyone did!

Former member, RCAF (WD)

"Will you thumb for us?"

Once when my friend and I were out on a pass, we were walking along the side of the road and just ahead of us were these two airmen. One of them said to us, "Hey, girls! We can't get a ride. If we hide in the ditch will you thumb for us?" Well, the very next car that came along screeched to a halt for us Wrens and then out jumped these two fellows and hopped into the car instead of us. We got quite a laugh out of it, too.

Former member, WRCNS

Cpl. Wilma Williamson, CWAC, using searchlight as a mirror, Ottawa, May 1944.

Usherettes!

On a weekend pass three of us decided to go down to New York City – complete with our CANADA badges on our shoulders. We weren't really supposed to do that because it was reserved for people serving overseas; but we were going to the States and we thought we'd better identify ourselves. Well, we did that alright, but it didn't work out quite the way we'd expected. We went to a matinee at the Met and someone mistook the three of us – standing there in our uniforms – for usherettes!

Former member, RCAF (WD)

Sixteen baths a day

Sometimes on a forty-eight-hour pass we'd go over to Buffalo, N.Y., and stay at the Statler Hotel there and take about sixteen baths a day. Then we'd go out shopping and buy sexy nightgowns trimmed with lace – and fancy bedroom slippers. After we'd reported back, we'd float around the barracks in our new outfits letting off steam before we had to get back into uniform the next morning bright and early.

Former member, RCAF (WD)

"Whatcha doin' with them there 'Wrens'?"

We were in this little general store – the kind with a big pot-bellied stove and a whole cluster of fishermen sitting around. They got to talking to my friend and me, and one of these old boys invited us home for supper. Since we were on leave, we decided we might as well accept his offer of hospitality – until we came to his house. In the doorway stood the biggest woman I've ever seen with her arms folded and the next thing I knew she was calling out to her husband, "Whatcha doin' with them there Wrens?" She'd scared us half to death before we figured out that she was only kidding. As it turned out, they were the kindest, most generous couple in the world. They put us up for the night and the next morning – before dawn – he had us up to go out fishing and I caught a dandy big fish. For the rest of our time down there, we ended up staying with them whenever we got time off.

Former member, WRCNS

Real pusser rum

In Digby one Christmas Day some of us were out walking. There were very few restaurants open and out of the blue this British naval officer came up and started talking to us. Well, we ended up having Christmas dinner on board this British sub. We weren't the only women. There were a few other Wrens and that was the first time I ever tasted real "pusser rum" . . . It turned out to be one of the happiest Christmases we'd ever spent!

I met this wonderful fellow while I was down East. He was training to be a naval gunner and one night he said to me, "I don't think I'm really cut out for killing." When he wrote his exams, he deliberately failed them so he could get out. I'm still not quite sure how he managed it, but he went

Canadian Forces Photographic Unit, DND, PL-8977

Airwoman Frances Duncan makes use of her standard overseas issue "sit up and beg" bicycle, June 1942.

to the States and joined the Medical Corps. I guess that's what he really wanted to do, but when he left it was very hard, because I'd become very fond of him. When I saw him off at the station, I wondered if we'd ever see each other again; and, as things turned out, it was nearly forty years before we did meet again.

Former member, WRCNS

"Sit up and beg" bikes

Having grown up in the Depression, I'd never ridden a bike. My brother had one but I didn't and none of my girlfriends did either. So when I got to England, it was a choice of learning how to ride a bike or walking a mile to the mess hall. We were actually issued with bikes, "sit-up-and-beg" bikes – they called them. Finally, I got a bike of my own and we used to go for miles, sometimes forty miles in a day. It kept us from feeling too isolated if we could get into town.

Former member, RCAF (WD)

Wrong for me to be in uniform

My parents lived in a small town – very much removed from the war – and I got the impression when I'd be home on leave that some people thought it was wrong for me to be in uniform. I almost felt as if they thought of me as a prostitute or something. They hardly seemed to realize there was a war on, some of them.

Former member, WRCNS

Driven by a madman

I remember being driven to our barracks up in Torbay and I thought we were being driven by a madman, because he was driving on the wrong side of the road. We'd all forgotten, of course, that in Newfoundland they were still part of England and so he was simply doing what any good Englishman would do by keeping to the left.

Even with a three-day pass, where was there to go, with no buses and no trains? You could get a taxi and go for a little excursion for an afternoon but mainly we were just stuck there and left to make the best of it . . . We'd get movies on the base and if you wanted to go out for dinner the menu was pretty limited – mainly fish! Thank goodness we were allowed to fraternize with the Americans who were stationed up there. My whole social life depended on them and I guess they were as happy to have us there as we were to have them to go out with. Towards the end most people were just itching to get out of there and on with their lives.

Former member, RCAF (WD)

Put on some music

The only time we ever heard anything about the war was when we went home on a pass. If the news came on in the barracks, somebody would just come along and switch the station and put on some music. We really didn't want to hear about it much. We all knew that when the war was over they'd tell us about it and then we could all go home.

Former member, RCAF (WD)

Molly Lamb Bobak, *Waiting in Edmonton*, February 1943.

SEVEN

Phasing Out

B Y LATE 1944 THE CONCEPT of women in uniform within the military had become more acceptable. Their presence was no longer a novelty and, in most quarters, they were regarded as a distinctly positive addition to morale. Following an inspection tour, the adjutant-general, Major-General Letson, observed that "the presence of women has raised the tone in the mess." The men, it seemed, were more apt to brush and comb their hair, curse less, eat with forks instead of knives, and sit up at the table instead of bending over their plates to shovel in the grub.[1]

On the other hand, the time was fast approaching when the recruitment of women into the services would become less than a priority. With the discontinuance of the Commonwealth Air Training Plan, all outstanding RCAF (WD) recruiting quotas were cancelled. Those interested in remaining in uniform were extended a warm welcome by the CWAC – which was more than delighted to enlist women who were "well-trained, experienced and patriotic."[2]

Despite the assurance of ready acceptance, records indicate that a disappointing number of WDs availed themselves of the opportunity to remain in uniform as members of the CWAC. In fact, by early 1945, the CWAC itself had begun taking steps to prepare its personnel for an impending return to civilian life. At a conference of commanding officers held in Ottawa, February 6–8, 1945, the corps was encouraged to employ the interim period to best advantage by providing educational and

CWAC Lt. Entwistle with her mother, Mrs. R. Entwistle, and her sister, Mrs. Al Saunders (right), after receiving medal, Ottawa, Ont.

vocational opportunities for its personnel. It was further suggested that the emphasis on military training should be reduced in favour of increased emphasis on civilian activities and the provision of instructional staff.[3]

The minister of national defence, General McNaughton, who was present at the conference, was clearly impressed by "the calibre of the Corps and the quality of work done" as well as by "the smartness of dress and deportment," which reflected inner principles and was a credit to the CWAC. Women in the service had put men "on their toes."[4]

It was noted with some pride at a later conference that the number of women taking advantage of the courses and lectures offered was well in excess of those in "the male Army." Speakers were brought in on a regular basis from such organizations as the Better Business Bureau as well as the Department of Public Health ("Care of Mother and Baby"), the VON, and the Visiting Homemakers. The T. Eaton Company offered the services of a knowledgeable employee willing to present talks on the selection of civilian clothing and budgeting a clothing allowance.

National Archives of Canada, PA-128258

Miss Mary Birchall modelling lime-green spun-rayon dress, suggested for purchase as part of CWAC discharge clothing allowance of $100, Glebe Collegiate, Ottawa, Ont., October 23, 1945.

At Trinity Barracks, Toronto, a "rehabilitation wing" was opened in January 1945 to begin processing women who would be demobilized in that particular military district – one of twelve such districts operating under the direction of the CWAC across Canada. But whether it was in Toronto or Calgary or in London, England, the phasing-out process for those awaiting discharge was far from uncomplicated. According to CWAC procedural directions for the Trinity Barracks Rehabilitation Wing, the receipt of clearance papers was merely the first of a long series of twelve interviews and examinations that included X-rays, a medical examination, psychological assessment, and a dental appointment (with all possible dental work to be completed before discharge). The ninth interview – with a civilian veterans' welfare officer – involved discussion of future plans in civilian life and an outline of courses and opportunities available.[5]

On discharge (honourable only!) CWAC personnel were permitted to keep one complete uniform. This, however, created a few unforeseen problems. One CWAC officer reported in alarm that:

> A few discharged personnel take advantage of having this uniform and wear it to obtain privileges only granted personnel *in* the Services. There are, among those discharged, a certain number of girls who, while in the Service, were a disgrace to the Corps from the moral standpoint. This type should not be permitted to retain the King's uniform on returning to civilian life.[6]

Another CWAC company commander put in a request for the automatic discharge of married personnel unless a desire to remain in the service was indicated: "Retaining a married Volunteer in the Corps against her will is detrimental and is reflected in the Volunteer's work. It also affects those working with her . . . Her loyalties are divided and she is not a good soldier."[7]

Undoubtedly the other two women's services were experiencing similar frustrations of one sort and another. However, following the jubilant news in early May 1945 that Victory in Europe had at long last been secured, Commander Adelaide Sinclair sent this message to all WRCNS personnel overseas:

All members of the Women's Royal Canadian Naval Service will rejoice in the news that Victory in Europe has been won. It may be hard to grasp the full cost of that victory in terms of human lives, human sufferings and unbelievable devastation. That some of this can cease is indeed an event to celebrate, but it should be a celebration of thankfulness rather than frivolity.

To have served with the Navy and to have contributed to its share in this victory will always be a proud recollection for each of us. All of us have received more from these associations than we shall ever be able to give in return. We must remember now that the total war is still not won and that our work continues as long as we are needed. It may require added efforts to maintain our present standards to the end – but that we must do. Our responsibility as citizens will not cease with the coming of peace. If the post-war world is to be worthy of the sacrifices of past years, it will need the continued effort in peace of the women who have proved their usefulness in war.[8]

RCAF (WD)s lining up in front of London HQ for Victory Parade, May 1945.

Canadian Forces Photographic Unit, DND, PL-94395

Within a few months, the August 1945 surrender of the Japanese in the Pacific brought an end to the "total war" and the process of "total rehabilitation" began in earnest. In the interval between the entry of the first female recruits in the autumn of 1941 and the cessation of hostilities, 244 Canadian servicewomen had been awarded military decorations, ranging from Mention in Despatches to an M.B.E.

They and their thousands of other compatriots in uniform who had answered the call of duty had "done their bit." The time had come for them to get on with their lives, to return home to build a future full of hope and promise.

Notebook

"I don't have to be a housewife"

During the war we did everything a man could do except fight, and after it was all over there was a lot of unrest as well as happiness and sadness, all mixed in together. Some women were saying to themselves, "I don't really want to have children. I don't have to be a housewife. I want my own freedom, now, because I've proved that I'm as smart as any other person

Photo by Barney J. Gloster. National Archives of Canada, PA-152513

Piper Flossie Ross of the CWAC Pipe Band on deck of a German "E" Boat. The Pipe Band toured units of the Canadian Occupation Army, Wilhelshaven, Germany, October 4, 1945.

. . . So if people did marry, they had a different outlook, because they were different women than they had been before the war. And they raised a different generation of children because of it.

Former member, RCAF (WD)

Such a long wait
Towards the end, a lot of what we were doing was basically make-work, catch-up kind of stuff. It really didn't seem to have a great deal of importance at that stage in the war and it certainly contributed to a degree of restlessness. No one had felt that way while things were hanging in the balance, as they had been for such a long time. But once it was all over the wait to get out of Newfoundland seemed endless. The isolation had really taken its toll.

Former member, RCAF (WD)

Feeling really lost
I had a good job waiting for me when I got out, but some of my friends were scared to death of getting back into civilian life. Being in the service meant that everything was decided for you. You didn't have to think. You knew what you were going to wear and where you were going to eat and the whole routine was laid out. So a lot of people were feeling really lost when they got out, because they weren't used to thinking for themselves.

Former member, WRCNS

Divine retribution – garbage detail
We started stocking up on liquor towards the end of the war, because we knew it was coming. We had orders to keep on working until official word came from Ottawa. Finally it arrived and out came all the bottles that had been stashed away. That night I drank Grand MacNish Scotch out of a huge wide-mouthed olive jar in the barracks. Anyone who could get home within a reasonable time was given a forty-eight-hour pass and the rest of us were asked to stay and man the station. Unfortunately I drew breakfast mess hall duty for the next morning and after the Grand MacNish and quantities of beer, I was feeling like the last rose of summer. I hadn't even taken off my hat and gloves from the night before and to top it off they told me I was on garbage detail – scraping plates. Divine retribution!

Former member, RCAF (WD)

To see the King and Queen and the princesses
A group of us walked to Buckingham Palace to see the King and Queen and the princesses on the balcony. The crowd was so great that it was literally impossible to move. If you'd fainted, there wouldn't have been any place to fall. The buses and the underground were completely jammed, so we ended up walking home as well. On the way somebody saw an admiral pushing a Wren in a wheelbarrow. He'd apparently lost a bet of some kind.

Former officer, CWAC

When all the lights were on again
In London we spent quite a lot of time underground. We'd come out of HQ and get on the "Tube" in the dark. Everything was blacked out, so you almost had to feel your way along. That first night when all the lights were on again, we came to our Tube station, the one we'd been going into for nearly two years, and we scarcely knew where we were.

Former member, RCAF (WD)

Photo by J.C.M. Hayward, Halifax, N.S. Private collection

Farewell to "WRENS" at HMCS Stadacona, March 12, 1946.

Numb from the knees down

Just the night before VE-Day, I met my husband. He'd just been released from prison camp. It had been a very hot day and after work I was persuaded to go across the street to the pub (Molly's). All they had left was beer and gin so I had a "Dog's Nose" – a shot of gin followed by beer. The effect was almost immediate. I was numb from the knees down and just then, in walked these two Canadian fellows to meet someone we both knew and that's how we met. About two weeks later we were engaged . . . The women I felt really sorry for were the ones left at home while their husbands were overseas. Not many marriages can stand three, four, five years of separation. There were many, many breakups after the war, I'm afraid.

Former officer, CWAC

I'd done my bit and that was it

The minute the war was over, I wanted out. My attitude was that I'd done my bit and that was it. I couldn't imagine being in the service in peacetime.

It would seem so meaningless. . . And as it was, I thought I'd never get out. It took forever. They took all the girls that were married off the draft first; next came the girls that were in "non-essential" trades; and then there was me. By the time I got discharged, the station was like a deserted village.

Former member, RCAF (WD)

Such a strange order!

In Halifax, after the riots following VE-Day, they decided they'd better be organized in order to prevent trouble when VJ-Day came along. Our orders were to make sure no one on the grounds was sitting or lying down. Such a strange order! But they thought that as long as they kept everybody in motion and gave them all they wanted to eat and drink, things would be contained. So, along with the shore patrol, we worked in six-hour shifts, looking under hedges and bushes for bodies that were disobeying orders ... In all of Halifax there were only three or four restaurants. There was one called the Green Lantern (better known as the Green Latrine), and another one which was very famous for seafood. During the riots, that was one of the few places with its windows left intact, because they were smart enough to stay open and keep on cooking and serving food all night long.

Former officer, WRCNS

After all those years of powdered eggs

When we were on our way home, we went down to Southampton from London and by the time we got on board we were ravenous. It was the *Ile de France*, with a French crew, and when they put white bread and rolls and butter on the table it was gone within seconds ... Then, on the train coming from Halifax, there was bacon and eggs. What a thrill after all those years of powdered eggs!

There was a bunch of prisoners coming back with us on board ship – Canadian prisoners – fellows who'd gotten themselves in hot water over there and were on their way home. Somebody would come up and whisper in your ear, "I don't think you should be talking to him. He's doing so many months for armed robbery," or whatever. Most of them probably hadn't done much more than rob a few meters, but we weren't allowed on deck after sundown. For our own protection, I suppose.

Former officer, CWAC

She hung on to my hand all the way

I think probably the saddest experience I had came at the end of the war when we were meeting the trains. You'd take one look at some of the guys and turn away. It was too much to bear looking at them and the nursing sisters coming back from Hong Kong – some of them with their tongues cut out and some pregnant . . . I drove one of them to the military hospital in Kingston and I often used to drop around and visit her on my rounds. She was one of the ones who'd had her tongue cut out. When they were transferring her to London, Ontario, she refused to go unless I drove her. That morning she wrote a note asking me what kind of cigarettes I smoked. I told her and then she handed me some money and wrote that I should get myself some. She sat up in front with me all the way, even though she wasn't supposed to, and every time I put a cigarette out, she'd have another one waiting for me . . . At one point we went to a restaurant and, of course she had a hard time eating. Maybe it was the drive or maybe it was nervousness, but she was sick all over everything and you could tell she was dreadfully embarrassed, poor thing. Then when we got to the hospital she hung on to my hand all the way to her room . . . To this day I feel bad that I never went back there to visit, because I'd promised I would.

Former member, CWAC

So we decided to wait

My husband, who was a doctor, and Jewish, told me before he went overseas that we'd be married after the war, if we won. (If we'd lost, goodness knows what would have become of him – being Jewish.) So we decided to wait. As it turned out he was taken prisoner in '42 and was in the Japanese camp on the River Kwai. For three years all I got was a few postcards. That was all the word I had and he had absolutely no word from me. All that would be written on the card would be, "I am well. I am employed," with greetings to So-and-so and that's all the mail they could send out . . . We were married twelve days after he returned.

Former officer, WRCNS

The day they dropped the Bomb

I was on draft to go overseas when my fiancé came back from the Netherlands to go to the Pacific war. If you were marrying someone going there, you were given an extra month's leave. So we were married in

Canadian Forces Photographic Unit, DND, PL-36813

A joyful reunion.

Vancouver on August sixth – the day they dropped the Bomb. And that was that!

Former member, CWAC

Farming and animal husbandry

We were all asked to attend a meeting to ask us what we wanted to do in civilian life. I suggested that I'd like to own a castle in Rumania, which wasn't a very popular answer. I was fixed by a steely stare by our senior officer . . . It seems there was a farm adjacent to the station and the land belonged to the Ministry of Transport, so someone decided it would be a very good idea to get some animals and then people who were interested could learn all about farming and animal husbandry. Every creature we bought had a different ailment before long; and generally, the plan was not the success it was intended to be.

Former member, RCAF (WD)

A lot of us just blew it

For ten years or so after the war, depending on how long you'd been in the service, you could buy a piece of land (or whatever) much cheaper but a lot of us just blew it. The smart ones were the ones who used the opportunity to go on with their education through the DVA [Department of Veterans' Affairs]. To my mind, though, this wasn't publicized very well – what was available to you as a veteran – at least not right away. I think if it had been promoted better, a lot of people would have done a lot of things differently.

Former member, CWAC

Things they never would have dreamed of

The experience of having been in uniform was very rewarding for a lot of people. They ended up doing all sorts of things that they probably would never have dreamed of before the war . . . I remember one girl on our station who was an airframe mechanic – one of the few women in that trade. She passed all her trade tests with flying colours, which irritated some of the men, because they had to try theirs several times before making it . . . I think her Air Force experience expanded her life in a way that it wouldn't have been otherwise.

Former member, RCAF (WD)

It changed everyone

It was quite a shock when you left the service. When it was all over. It was an unforgettable experience and I certainly have no regrets. It changed everyone. You'd been protected in the service. Everything was part of a routine and there was a lot of adjusting to do afterwards, for women as well as for men. I don't think some of the men ever adjusted, for that matter. There were a lot of divorces after the war because of it. Everything had changed!

Former member, CWAC

I was nobody again

During the war I felt like I was somebody, I was recognized, and then it

Canadian Forces Photographic Unit, DND, PL-20839

RCAF (WD) photographers M. Dudlyke of Lea Park, Alta., M. Clayborne of Truro,
N.S., and Jeanne Farris of Fredericton, N.B., cross the tarmac at dawn, accompanied
by Flt. Sgt. A.D. Lang.

was all over and I was nobody again. My family didn't seem to care what
I'd done. I was just supposed to forget all that and fit in. It wasn't quite
that simple.

Former member, RCAF (WD)

Like having a language of your own
Having shared that experience was like having a language of your own
that all of you could understand. I was most conscious of it, I think, just
after the war, when I got out of uniform and went to university. It was
really hard to connect with my fellow students, who hadn't been through
what I had. They were living in a totally different world. I only survived
because I was able to spend all my free time with my friends from the
service ... I thought about things differently and reacted to things
differently. It's hard to say exactly why this was. All I know is that it was
very different. I guess you could call it part of the postwar letdown.
Things would never be the same again...

Former member, RCAF (WD)

NOTES

Introduction

1. G.W. Nicholson, *Canada's Nursing Sisters*. Canadian War Museum/ National Museums of Canada, Historical Publication 13 (Toronto: Samual Stevens, Hakkert, 1975).
2. Ibid.
3. Lt. Col. L.J. Davis, *Employment of Women in Canada's Armed Forces Past and Present* (Department of National Defence HQ, 1966).
4. *The Varsity*, Magazine Supplement (University of Toronto, 1916), Ontario Archives.
5. Ibid.
6. "The Canadian Red Cross Society Record of Four Years' Service," *The Canadian Gazette*, September 26, 1916, Ontario Archives.
7. *Imperial Munitions Board of Canada, 1916. Women in the Production of Munitions in Canada*, Ontario Archives.

Chapter 1: Onward and Upward

1. *The Canadian Women's Army Corps*, File #156-130, Department of National Defence, Directorate of History, Ottawa.
2. J.M. Cowper, *The ATS* (London: The War Office, 1949), pp. 2–8.
3. Miss Henrietta Rea, Victoria, B.C.
4. Ibid.
5. Robert Collins, *They Also Served*, File # 1350-500, Department of National Defence, Directorate of History, Ottawa, December 1968.
6. RCAF (WD) File, November 8, 1939, December 16, 1939, Department of National Defence, Directorate of History, Ottawa.
7. RCAF (WD) File, Memo, May 14, 1941, Department of National Defence, Directorate of History, Ottawa.
8. File #120, Department of National Defence, Directorate of History, Ottawa.

9. Ibid.
10. Miss Henrietta Rea, Victoria, B.C.
11. R.10-32, Letter dated February 1941, Department of National Defence, Directorate of History, Ottawa.
12. Hansard, July 3, 1940.
13. CWAC (1941–1946) Report #15, Department of National Defence, Directorate of History, Ottawa.
14. File #156-013(01) Appendix A, Department of National Defence, Directorate of History, Ottawa.
15. File #120, Letter dated July 5, 1941, Department of National Defence, Directorate of History, Ottawa.

Chapter 2: Joining Up
1. File #181-003, Department of National Defence, Directorate of History, Ottawa.
2. Dr. Jean Cottam, *Soviet Women in Combat and Support Forces (1941–45)* (Ottawa: Department of National Defence).
3. File #391-009 (D36), CWAC Mobile Recruiting Reports, November 19, 1943, Department of National Defence, Directorate of History, Ottawa.
4. File #112.3M3009 (D112), CWAC Training, August 1942–October 1943, Department of National Defence, Directorate of History, Ottawa.
5. Letter from Ernest Lapointe, MP, October 2, 1941, Department of National Defence, Directorate of History, Ottawa.
6. Geneviève Auger and Raymonde Lamothe, *De la poêle à frire à la ligne de feu: La vie quotidienne des Québécoises pendant la guerre '39 – '45* (Montreal: Boréal Express, 1981).
7. Ibid.
8. File #113-3A 2009 (D1), Secret and Confidential Report on CWAC Recruits, "Why Women Join and How They Like It," Department of National Defence, Directorate of History, Ottawa.
9. Elliott-Haynes Research, Montreal, Toronto.
10. Ibid.
11. Letter to the Secretary of National Defence for Air, June 4, 1943, Department of National Defence, Directorate of History, Ottawa.
12. Letter from J.A. Sully, Air Vice-Marshal, for the Chief of Air Staff, August 29, 1942, Department of National Defence, Directorate of History, Ottawa.

Chapter 3: Preparing to Serve

1. Rosamond Greer, *The Girls of the King's Navy* (Victoria, B.C.: Sono Nis Press, 1983).
2. DND Memorandum, Major-General H.T.C. Letson, Adjutant General, October 22, 1942, Department of National Defence, Directorate of History, Ottawa.
3. DND HQ Memorandum, June 8, 1943, Department of National Defence, Directorate of History, Ottawa.
4. File #818.009, D 4315, Department of National Defence, Directorate of History, Ottawa.
5. Ibid.
6. Ibid.
7. Ibid.
8. File #181.009, CWAAF Training (October–December 1941), Department of National Defence, Directorate of History, Ottawa.
9. Ibid.
10. Memorandum 426-12 (D of M), May 18, 1942.
11. Press Release, DND Public Relations (Army), August 15, 1941.
12. File #113.3C1 (D1), Letter to Mme. Thérèse Casgrain, Department of National Defence, Directorate of History, Ottawa.
13. Ibid.
14. Memorandum HQ 54-27-9-77 (Meds), July 13, 1943, Department of National Defence, Directorate of History, Ottawa.
15. File # 818.009, Department of National Defence, Directorate of History, Ottawa

Chapter 4: All in Together, Girls

1. File #181.003 (1465), Department of National Defence, Directorate of History, Ottawa.
2. Ibid.
3. DND HQ Memorandum 54-27-11-17 (Meds/bf), July 24, 1944, Department of National Defence, Directorate of History, Ottawa.
4. Memorandum to Minister of Defence Ralston, June 6, 1942, Microfilm #866-CWAC C 4989, Public Archives of Canada.
5. Minutes of meeting with Major-General Knox, CWAC Files, October 24, 1942, Department of National Defence, Directorate of History, Ottawa.

6. DND (Army) Memorandum to Officers Commanding CWAC, March 21, 1944, Department of National Defence, Directorate of History, Ottawa.
7. RCAF (WD) File #181.003 (1465), Department of National Defence, Directorate of History, Ottawa.
8. Army HQ Form 8972 (Meds/9h), May 31, 1943.
9. Ibid.
10. File #181.003, RCAF (WD), Memorandum for Chief of Air Staff, June 6, 1942, Department of National Defence, Directorate of History, Ottawa.
11. File #181.009 (D 35530), Department of National Defence, Directorate of History, Ottawa.
12. RCAF (WD) Training Syllabus for Officers, Lecture #6: Hygiene and Welfare.
13. Report #68, Army Headquarters, Historical Section G 5, June 17, 1954.
14. Army Headquarters Memorandum 54-27-11-17 (Meds/bf), July 24, 1944.
15. Ibid.
16. File #325.009 (D252), Department of National Defence, Directorate of History, Ottawa.
17. File #181.009 (D3553) RCAF (WD), Department of National Defence, Directorate of History, Ottawa.
18. File #325.009 (D252), Department of National Defence, Directorate of History, Ottawa.

Chapter 5: On Duty at Home and Overseas
1. File #120, Vol. 2, CWAC Overseas, Department of National Defence, Directorate of History, Ottawa.
2. Memo #8081, December 5, 1942, Canadian Military Headquarters, London.
3. *The Rally*, January 1943, London.
4. File #120, Appendix B, CWAC Overseas, Department of National Defence, Directorate of History, Ottawa.
5. File #181.002 (D423), Department of National Defence, Directorate of History, Ottawa.
6. G.N. Tucker, "The Naval Service of Canada: Its Official History" (Ottawa: King's Printer, 1952).

Chapter 7: Phasing Out

1. File #113.3C1.(D.1), Department of National Defence, Directorate of History, Ottawa.
2. CWAC HQ Memo 54-27-58-4, November 24, 1944, Ottawa.
3. File #115.1009 (D.22), Department of National Defence, Directorate of History, Ottawa.
4. Ibid.
5. File #325.009 (252), Department of National Defence, Directorate of History, Ottawa.
6. Ibid.
7. File #115.1009 (D.22), Department of National Defence, Directorate of History, Ottawa.
8. File #112.21009 (D.163), Department of National Defence, Directorate of History, Ottawa.

RELATED SOURCES

Auger, Geneviève, and Raymonde Lamothe. *De la poêle à frire à la ligne de feu: La vie quotidienne des Québécoises pendant la guerre '39 – '45.* Montreal: Boréal Express, 1981.

Bobak, Molly Lamb. *Wild Flowers of Canada.* Toronto: Pergamon Press, 1978.

Bikin, Martin, and Shirley Bach, *Women in the Military.* Washington, D.C.: Brookings Institute, 1977.

Bowman, Phyllis. *We Skirted the War!* Prince Rupert, B.C.: P. Bowman, 1975.

Brittain, Vera. *Testament of Youth: An Autobiographical Study of the Years 1900–1925.* London: Virago, 1978 (first published in 1933).

Broadfoot, Barry. *Six War Years, 1939–1945: Memories of Canadians at Home and Abroad.* Toronto: Doubleday, 1974.

Bechles, Gordon. *Canada Comes to England.* London: Hodder, Bechles, Wison & Stoughton, 1941.

Bruce, Jean. *Back the Attack! Canadian Women During the Second World War – At Home and Abroad.* Toronto: Macmillan of Canada, 1985.

Collins, Robert. "When Canadian Women Went to War." *Star Weekly Magazine*, September 23, 1961.

Conrod, W. Hugh. *Athene, Goddess of War: The Canadian Women's Army Corps – Their Story.* Dartmouth, N.S.: Writing and Editorial Services, 1984.

Douglas, W.A.B., and Brereton Greenhous. *Out of the Shadows: Canada in the Second World War.* Toronto: Oxford University Press, 1977.

Drummond, J.D. *Blue For Girl: The Story of the WRENS.* London: Allen Publishers, 1960.

Eaton, Lt.-Col Margaret. "The Canadian Women's Army Corps." *Canadian Geographical Journal* 27 (December 1943): 278–85.

Ellis, Jean M., with Isabel Dingman. *Facepowder and Gunpowder.* Toronto: S.J. Reginald Saunders and Co. Ltd., 1947.

German, Tony. *The Sea at Our Gates.* Toronto: McClelland & Stewart, 1990.

Granatstein, J.L. *Canada's War: The Politics of the Mackenzie King Government, 1939–1945.* Toronto: Oxford University Press, 1975.

Gravel, Jean-Yves. *Le Québec et la Guerre.* Montreal: Boréal Express, 1974.

Greer, Rosamond "Fiddy." *The Girls of the King's Navy.* Victoria, B.C.: Sono Nis Press, 1983.

Hannon, Leslie F. *Canada at War.* Canadian Illustrated Library. Toronto: McClelland & Stewart, 1968.

Hatch, F. *Medical Research and Development in the Canadian Army during World War II, 1942–1946.* Toronto: University of Toronto Press, 1968.

Hibbert, Joyce, ed. *The War Brides.* Toronto: Peter Martin, 1978.

King, Alison. *Golden Wings.* N.Y., London: White Lion Publishers, 1975 (originally published in 1956).

Moore, Mary Macleod. "Canadian Women War Workers Overseas." *Canadian Magazine*, January 1919.

Morton, Desmond. *Canada and War: A Military and Political History.* Toronto: Butterworths, 1981.

Pope, Maurice A. *Soldiers, Politicians: The Memoirs of Lt.-General Maurice A. Pope.* Toronto: University of Toronto Press, 1962.

Powley, A.E. *Broadcast from the Front: Canadian Radio Overseas during World War II.* Publication #11. Toronto: Canadian War Museum, Hakkert, 1975.

Nicholson, G.W.L. *Canada's Nursing Sisters.* Historical Publication 13. Canadian War Museum, National Museums of Canada. Toronto: Samuel Stevens, Hakkert, 1975.

Pierson, Ruth Roach. *"They're Still Women After All" : The Second World War and Canadian Womanhood.* Toronto: McClelland and Stewart, 1986.

Prentice, Alison, et al. *Canadian Women: A History.* Toronto: Harcourt Brace Jovanovich, 1988.

Robertson, Heather. *A Terrible Beauty: The Art of Canada at War.* Toronto: James Lorimer and Co., 1977.

Robson Roe, Kathleen. *War Letters from the C.W.A.C.* Toronto: Kakabeka Publishing Co., 1975.

Rupp, Leila J. *Mobilizing Women for War: German and American Propaganda, 1939–1945.* Princeton: Princeton University Press, 1978.

Saywell, Shelley. *Women in War.* Toronto: Viking, 1985.

Sinclair, Commander Adelaide. "Women's Royal Canadian Naval Service." *Canadian Geographical Journal* 27 (December 1943): 286–91.

Stacey, C.P. *Arms, Men and Governments: The War Policies of Canada, 1939–1945.* Ottawa: Queen's Printer, 1970.

Van Wagenen Keil, Sally. *The Magnificent Women in Their Flying Machines* (History of U.S. Women's Airforce Service Pilots). New York: Rawson, Wade Publishers, 1979.

Walker, Wing Officer Willa. "Royal Canadian Air Force (W.D.)." *Canadian Geographical Journal* 27 (December 1943): 268–75.

Whitton, Charlotte E. *Canadian Women in the War.* Toronto: Macmillan, 1942.

Ziegler, Mary. *We Serve That Men May Fly: The Story of the Women's Division, Royal Canadian Air Force.* Hamilton: RCAF (WD) Association, 1973.